PUBLIC SERVICES:

WORKING FOR
THE CONSUMER

"La transformation des relations entre l'administration et les administres ... s'explique ... par ... la contagion de l'esprit consumeriste..." **France, 1988 (84)**

"The Swedish public administration is in a period of change ... less bureaucracy and better service ... (C)itizens must assume greater influence as consumers of the public services..." **Sweden, 1989 (71)**

"Públicos e servicos públicos — uma nova relação" **Portugal, 1988 (132)**

" 'Serving the Country Better'... In the delivery of service to the public ... recognition of the primacy of the customer must be paramount". **Ireland, 1985 (85)**

" 'Bedarfsgerechte und bürgernahe öffentliche Dienstleistungen' steht in dem großen Zusammenhang, der mit dem Begriff 'Verbesserung des Verhältnisses zwischen Bürgern und Verwaltung gekennzeichnet ist. In der Bundesrepublik Deutschland ist dieser Begriff von Bund, Ländern und Gemeinden als Ziel der Politik anerkannt." **Germany, 1989 (96)**

"1987 is the year of the customer". **Delft Municipal Government (141)**

"Una dinámica de presión sobre la Administración en exigencia de que los servicios publicos sean prestados con ... receptividad...'mejor servicio a la clientela'.." **Spain, 1988 (108)**

"...the consumer dimension...is in danger of becoming...'the flavour of the month'." **UK, 1987 (123)**

PUBLIC SERVICES:

WORKING FOR THE CONSUMER

A review of initiatives in Europe to improve the responsiveness of public services to consumers

Joyce Epstein
RICA, London

European Foundation
for the Improvement of
Living and Working Conditions
Loughlinstown House, Shankill,
Co. Dublin, Ireland

This booklet is also available in the following languages:

ES ISBN 92-826-0325-3
DA ISBN 92-826-0326-1
DE ISBN 92-826-0327-X
GR ISBN 92-826-0328-8
FR ISBN 92-826-0330-X
IT ISBN 92-826-0331-8
NL ISBN 92-826-0332-6
PT ISBN 92-826-0333-4

Luxembourg: OFFICE FOR OFFICIAL
PUBLICATIONS OF THE
EUROPEAN COMMUNITIES 1990

Cataloguing data can be found at the end of this publication.

ISBN: 92-826-0329-6

Catalogue number: SY-58-90-950-EN-C

©Copyright: EUROPEAN FOUNDATION
FOR THE IMPROVEMENT OF
LIVING AND WORKING CONDITIONS, 1990.

For rights of translation or reproduction, application should be made to the Director, European Foundation for the Improvement of Living and Working Conditions, Louglinstown House, Shankill, Co. Dublin, Ireland.

Cartoons: Bob Fannin
Larry Parks
Harlow Council

Typesetting and Print Production:
Printset & Design Ltd., Dublin

Original language: English

Printed in Ireland

Preface

This review has been undertaken as a link between the Foundation's previous work on consumer issues, notably on information about urban services, and the development of future studies. It represents an effort to describe and order a large number of changes underway in public administrations, aimed at improving the service to users. It does not aim to cover all services or the public sector as a whole; it focuses upon services such as health, education, and, housing where there is direct worker-consumer contact; and it excludes transport, post and the utilities. It looks, in particular, at the relatively disadvantaged consumer in relation to these public services.

The Research and writing were done by Joyce Epstein and colleagues at the Research Institute for Consumer Affairs (London) and the project was co-ordinated by Robert Anderson at the Foundation. In addition to a biographical search of the international literature, field visits were made to look at examples of innovative practice; more than 100 officials were contacted from the central administrations and interested organisations, covering all countries of the European Community.

The starting point for the report is an analysis of deficiencies in current public services. This leads to presentation of initiatives designed to respond to current problems, accepting that perhaps not all these initiatives were undertaken in the name of "consumerism". Fourteen categories of development were illustrated ranging from improved public information and reception facilities to decentralisation, setting standards and consumer participation. Examples are drawn from nearly all countries of the European Community and a series of more detailed, though brief, case studies are presented.

The review points out that few of these initiatives have been subjected to systematic evaluation, and calls for more work on assessing service quality from the consumer point of view. This is the first of four types of systematic research outlined. Other proposals include work on the impact of consumer initiatives on the quality of life of consumers, and on the quality of working life for those who provide the services. As the structure and consumer-oriented provision in the public services change, there are likely to be implications for training, job organisation, ways of working and communication, and appropriate use of technology. These, too. need to be studied. An Evaluation meeting in Brussels attended by representatives of governments, trade unions, employers and the services of the European Commission offered other suggestions for research on transfer of initiatives, public/private partnerships and the relation between central and local authority responsibility for delivery of services.

At this stage in the development of the theme, the review gives an indication of the range of initiatives already underway, and points to some of the implications. It should assist those in administration and management, as well as representative organisations, to identify key issues for further work and analysis.

Clive Purkiss
Director

Eric Verborgh
Deputy Director

RICA (Research Institute for Consumer Affairs, 2 Marylebone Road, London NW1 4DX) was set up in 1961, by Consumers' Association, to conduct independent research on any consumer issue of public interest particularly where the needs of disadvantaged people are concerned. RICA research, both national and European, has ranged over a wide variety of topics, including equipment and transport for disabled people, shopping needs of the elderly, problems of children in hospital, and computerised information services for welfare claimants. RICA research is funded by government agencies, public trusts and foundations, and other bodies.

CONTENTS

PART ONE:	Introduction	9
PART TWO:	**Problems for Consumers of Public Services**	13
PART THREE:	**European Developments in Consumerism**	21
	Reception	22
	Information	25
	Simplification	27
	Coordination	28
	Marketing approach	31
	Complaints procedures	35
	Culture change	38
	Setting standards	40
	Decentralisation	46
	Personnel practices	49
	Two-way staff communication	53
	Accountability and autonomy	55
	Competition	58
	Consumer participation and representation	59
PART FOUR:	Discussion	69
PART FIVE:	**Summary and Conclusions**	83
APPENDIX—CASE STUDIES		89
BIBLIOGRAPHY		113

PART ONE

Introduction

Consumerism within the public sector has recently become a major preoccupation throughout Europe and, notwithstanding the last quote (above), continues to excite interest. Although consumer organisations in Europe have been championing consumer issues for many years in some parts of the public sector, it is only relatively recently that senior administrators within government itself have taken up the theme.

It is not possible to date the emergence of this new thinking from a single point in time, but one event does stand out. That was the 1982 publication in the US of the book, "In Search of Excellence" by Peters and Waterman. (121) Five years later, Hoggett and Hambleton noted that, "...much of the public sector is still reeling under the weight of books, seminars and training events which have been prompted by the publication of the seminal 'In Search of Excellence'." (82)

Peters and Waterman had examined private sector companies and discovered among other things that the most successful ones — the "excellent companies" — were those that were "close to the customer". The idea was picked up by the public sector, "excellent companies" became "excellent administrations" and the drive to remove barriers between the administration and the consumer was on.

Whom are we talking about?

Consumer, customer, client, user, citizen, public — all these terms, and more, have been used and the significance of each has been interminably argued over, in the so-far short history of public sector consumerism. In the British health service there has even been an attempt to coin a new word — "clipats" — to signify that people in hospital are both clients and patients (124). In France, some have ruled out the term "client" as completely inappropriate (84) while the French Prime Minister himself has declared those who use public services are indeed "clients" (2):

> **Un entretien avec M. Michel Rocard**
> L'« usager ». du service public devrait dans bien des cas devenir un « client »
> Comment mieux satisfaire les usagers du service public? Dans l'entretien que [...]tation et le dialogue. L'objectif du premier ministre est que les fonctionnaires et les [...]

In this paper we propose to stick generally to the term "consumer" while acknowledging that there are important issues implied e.g. by the broader term "citizen". Such issues will arise in the course of the paper.

What is consumerism?

Consumerism in the public sector has been described as "a bewildering variety of contrasting and sometimes contradictory notions"(123). Certainly "getting close to the customer" has been introduced into the public sector to achieve a variety of apparently wildly differing ends: to increase efficiency, cut costs, improve image, enhance international economic competitiveness, motivate staff, promote "new right" ideals of the market place, promote "old left" ideals of "power to the people", and more generally, improve the quality of public sector service. This paper will deal with such issues in succeeding sections, but here consumerism is defined as the adoption of a consumer-oriented philosophy of administration — to *serve* the public — and the introduction into the administration of various practical arrangements which will make services more responsive to consumer influence.

11

The main part of the paper, Section III, will focus on practical initiatives in consumerism, to describe what is actually happening under this banner across Europe. There are many new developments and in order to give an idea of the range of activities, each can be dealt with in this paper only briefly. The aim is not to analyse each area in depth, but to stimulate interest and further exploration of the subject. Section IV will discuss selected issues, and Section V will provide a summary and conclusions. This is followed by an appendix giving short case histories, to further illustrate individual developments. But first, Section II takes a very brief look at what the problems are in public service from the consumer point of view and looks at general reasons for those consumer problems.

PART TWO

Problems for Consumers of Public Sector Services

"When dispensing money or services, they (public officials) still manage to behave as though they have paid for them out of their own private pockets, not from the taxes of all the rest of us". (30)

The literature on public sector services and the consumer throughout Europe shows a remarkable consistency. Everywhere the issue has been examined — e.g. Ireland (85), UK (101), Spain (108), Italy (84), France (4), Germany (70), Sweden (72) — we find a similar pattern of consumer problems, which we briefly describe here using the categories adopted by consumer theorists to define the five requirements of consumerism: information, access, choice, redress, representation.

Information

Consumers, particularly those that come from disadvantaged sections of the community, lack information about the public services that are available. They do not know services exist, they do not understand their entitlements to services and they are confused about how to obtain services. Information that is given out is often couched in "officialese" and is totally incomprehensible to ordinary people. The complaint that "nobody tells me anything" ranks high on the list of consumer problems generated by research surveys.

Lack of consumer information, it should be emphasised, is not to be equated with lack of brochures, bulletins, etc; e.g. a recent study in France found there is so much written material that authorities there have had to produce "guides to guides". (84)

Access

Another all-too-common theme in consumer problems relates to the inaccessibility of public services. The issue of access covers a variety of problems — physical, social and institutional:

Physical access
Public services are often remote in both time and place. In many European states, public services shut down just at the very times that consumers can or wish to use them, e.g. at mid-day. One commentator refers to public sector "...visiting hours that seem fit only for leisurely retirees"(148). Distant locations (particularly in non-urban areas), forbidding buildings, confusing office lay-outs, hatches between staff and public, absence of adaptations for the disabled, have all been identified as contributing to the remoteness of public services.

Social access
The literature — both popular and research — has for years identified serious problems for consumers caused by what may be termed social barriers. Surveys have shown that consumers may too often feel they receive

impersonal, uncaring service (144), sometimes downright rude (49), delivered in an "authoritarian manner" (70) and as if all consumers were "des fraudeurs en puissance" (potential cheats) (84). A very recent study (9) shows that some public service staff still retain prejudices that there are "deserving" and "undeserving" poor. An evaluation in Spain said that it is difficult for consumers to feel a sense of active, willing help (84). Such problems of bureaucratic unhelpfulness have even become the subject of popular jokes and cartoons, but the problems are nonetheless real.

Institutional access
Complex rules and decision-making processes have also entered into the realm of folklore but,

> "...But I underestimated the bureaucracy. I rang the environmental health department.
> 'There's rats in Goscote. Could you give us some advice?'
> 'Oh, you speak to public works'. So I ring public works.
> 'Where are the rats?'
> 'Goscote'.
> 'No, are they above ground or below ground? If they're below ground they're our responsibility, if they're above, you'll have to ring the environmental health department'.
> 'You're kidding me'.
> 'No', they said 'that's the way it works'.
> I said, 'Whose responsibility is it if they're in the bloody roof — the RAF?'" (74)

again, the serious literature is filled with references: in Germany in 1986, 90 per cent of applications for unemployment benefit had to be sent back to applicants because the complexity of the rules reflected in the form made it totally impenetrable for consumers (39). Because of complex institutional compartmentalisation, consumers tend not to approach the right "bit" and have to withstand the frustrations of being referred, and possibly re-referred, "in a ping-pong administration in which they play the part of the ball" (4).

Choice

In the public service, choice too often means "take it or leave it". Consumers of public sector services have had little or none of the protection afforded by choice to consumers in the private sector. This built-in rigidity, identified as a problem for consumers in all countries studied (84), serves to exacerbate every other of the five consumer problem areas, but most particularly redress.

Redress

A recent study of public services in France concluded that, "administrations never apologise for or even recognise their mistakes ... rarely change a decision once taken" (84). In most countries studied, there is little opportunity for consumers to obtain redress in the public sector. The literature shows that complaints mechanisms, e.g. Ombudsmen, Mediateurs etc. are not well known to consumers and have a too-narrow remit anyway to be really useful. Furthermore, partly because of access barriers, most people with complaints tend not to voice them.

Representation

Consumers of public services must live with the consequences of decisions taken by public sector officials, but have little or no direct way of influencing the decision-making process. Complaints about "unjust and unfair services" (84) rank high in the list of European consumer problems in dealing with the public sector. This is clearly a complex issue and the discussion will be expanded in succeeding sections.

In summary then, public services from the consumer point of view can seem remote from and utterly unresponsive to the people they are intended to serve. Consumers often do not know what services are available. Services may be difficult to reach, intimidating to approach and surly to receive. Consumers feel — and are — excluded from the decision-making system, so that the services they get may not even be the ones they feel they want or need.

The public service has been the subject of many recent analyses that have tried to identify what it is about the system that makes it so lacking in orientation to the consumer, why it appears to the consumer, in the words of a French analyst, like a "gigantic, monolithic and impersonal block". (84)

Briefly, in order to control the distribution of resources in an impartial and objective way, public services have developed systems — rules and regulations — that can be administered in a standardised fashion. In order further to maintain control, government has created hierarchies within public sector employment whereby senior managers control middle managers, who control line staff, a hierarchy which encourages the system to orient inwards — each staff member answers to the next one above them, rather than to the consumer, i.e. to orient outwards.

This traditional hierarchical organisation of services — the pyramid structure — is perfectly suited to escaping all forms of public influence, control and evaluation. It applies rules and professional judgements from above in a standardised way, isolating the base of the pyramid from its local milieu, the consumer. "It mobilises the forces of inertia" (84).

The pyramid structure also hides accountability. Each official has to get his superior to approve decisions and

> "A group of inhabitants of a certain street in Amsterdam addressed a request to the local government. In addition to the traffic lights that were to be installed in a crossing nearby, they asked for a traffic-sign. They feared their street would be used as a stealth route. After the approval of the Department of Traffic/Police, the Department of General Affairs, and the Department of Traffic and Transport, the Public Service of Road Works was ordered to carry out the plan. And so it happened that three years after the expression of need, a civil servant appeared in the street in question. He carried a one-way traffic sign. However, he placed the sign at the wrong side of the road. Astonished inhabitants could not stop him from making that mistake. According to the plan on paper the man was carrying out his orders correctly. It took two more years before the mistake was corrected". (13)

thus is not held accountable for the service to the consumer.

The consumer almost by design becomes a very unimportant aspect of the system — a person to be circumvented rather than a customer to be served.

Those who have been working with public organisations (e.g. the Local Government Training Board in the UK) have discovered the enormity of the task involved in bringing about organisational change in the public service bureaucracy. There has not, until recently at any rate, been felt to be any great incentive for change. Things could keep ticking along pretty well as always, with consumers getting what they can out of the service, as best they can.

But change is coming. Public services are beginning to think about their public — "an attitude change on a scale akin to religious conversion" (109). In the next section we look at how this is being manifested.

A note on methodology: to discover what developments are taking place, we contacted senior administration officials in central government in every country of the European Community, and contacted those known to RICA to be interested in this subject among selected local government officials, non-governmental organisations, research institutes, consumer organisations, trade union representatives and elected politicians; over 100 contacts in all. Although the study is about member states of the EC, we also included some known developments in Sweden, Canada and the US, where relevant. In addition, we conducted a bibliographic search of the UK and international published literature in this area. A number of field visits were made to take a closer look at particular examples of innovative practice.

PART THREE

European Developments

Reception

Probably the most common initiative in consumer-oriented public service is to make improvements in the conditions of direct client/provider interface*. These include e.g. extended office hours for central government agencies in Ireland and in the Federal Republic of Germany, usually one late afternoon or evening per week. As part of a programme called the "politique de qualite totale", a prefecture in France has stopped the practice of mid-day closing, one of many such initiatives. In Italy in some local authorities, for example Modena, consumers can now ask for a meeting with staff outside normal opening hours if they have matters that cannot be solved otherwise.

Another development is to improve the quality of the premises. In the UK, under the Department of Social Security, some local offices have installed a range of amenities including magazines in the waiting room, children's toys, plants, paintings from the local art school, pleasing colour schemes, carpets, comfortable chairs, water and drinks dispensers, toilets, writing tables, nappy changing facilities, acoustic tiles, privacy screens. Such initiatives are published periodically in a book called "Service to the Public", which is distributed to all local office managers to encourage them to introduce their own improvements. It was found in at least one such refurbished social security office (in Leeds) that consumers value the improved environment and, significantly, two years later there had been no instances of vandalism or defacement, otherwise a chronic problem in social security offices.

Yet another development in improving reception arrangements focuses on the interpersonal relationship between counter staff and consumer. In one local authority in the UK for example (Tower Hamlets, in

---

*It should be noted that the categories of initiatives used in this report are not entirely separate. Many of the initiatives have elements that cut across categories or have several different purposes.

London), all staff having direct contact with the public, with special emphasis on housing and social services, are sent on a three-day course entitled "Customer Care". As a local politician responsible for the initiative said, "We want residents to feel they are being listened to sympathetically, not just fobbed off as fast as possible" (146).

Another aspect of improvement of relations is removing the anonymity, lessening the impersonal quality of public service. Many authorities at central and local level in e.g. Ireland, France and the UK are encouraging staff to wear name badges. This, however, is somewhat contentious. Although evaluation in the UK has shown that the "...public unanimously favoured name badges (because it) ensured approachability and encouraged them to be less tense..." (40), staff tend to remain apprehensive about it; in the UK social security office where evaluation took place, 20 per cent of staff in contact with the public refused to wear badges because they feared repercussions from the public. In two other social security offices where the situation was monitored, when staff wore name badges no problems ensued.

Better signs and a range of other reception arrangements to make the public service more open and accessible have also been introduced. For example a hospital in Paris (Broussais) has, as part of a larger project initiative called GIQ (Groupes Initiatives et Qualite) introduced colour-coded badges for different staff to allow better identification by patients of various functions and services. Receptionists ("Hotesses") have been introduced in many public agencies in France to provide information and guide people to the right "bit" of the office e.g. at the Prefecture in Lozere. In one local authority in the UK (Wrekin), the chief executive himself served at the town hall reception desk for about an hour every Monday morning to demonstrate the authority was really open to the customer. In similar vein, the chief executive of another local authority in the UK (Solihull) takes phone calls direct from the public for one hour in the morning every day of the week to show, "We are not faceless bureaucrats behind desks" (83).

There is a whole range of other activities that relate to improving the contact point between consumer and provider — everything from the requirement since 1986 in Spain to sign all official correspondence by name, to the lowering of reception desk heights in one local authority in the UK to make the office look less forbidding. All such initiatives have been dismissed by some critics as mere "tinkering", "cosmetic", "the smile school approach" to public service improvement, concerned more with the appearance, rather than the substance, of change.

But others make a strong case for the appearance of change, for adopting a commitment to action: it is important to be *doing* things, even small things, and to be seen to be doing them. Speaking at a seminar on consumers and public sector services in Bonn in 1987, a hospital general manager from the UK pointed out that such efforts as placing magazines, coffee and a television set in the waiting room have made the consumer happier, but also, perhaps more importantly, to have helped to change staff values and attitudes towards the consumers. It has stimulated them to "think consumer". "We are now confronting the issues of whether we are satisfying our customers, and if not, what are we going to do about it" (29). Going for early successes was seen in that hospital as a deliberate and strategic step to stimulate further change.

Information to consumers

Innovation in information provision was the subject of a recent RICA report for the European Foundation, "Providing Information about Urban Services" (51). It described in detail a framework for good practice in information-giving, and illustrated, with European examples, the characteristics of consumer-oriented information: information must be easily accessible, presented in an active and attractive way, using plain language that is easy to understand.

Improving the range and quality of information available to the public about health, social security and other services is a growing trend in consumer developments in the European Community, and has often been closely related to improvements in reception arrangements. For example, an important element of the hospital example, above, was that patients were not only made more comfortable while waiting, but they were also informed how long they would have to wait, and why. Another consumer survey of hospitals (129) showed that one of the major complaints people had was that "no one ever tells you how long you will have to wait" and people resent being made to feel that their time is less valuable than staff time.

Improved information to consumers — for example the series of leaflets issued in Spain, called "Passo a passo" (Step by step), which sets out in simple language the procedures to follow for various claims and services — may make services easier for the agency to deliver, by helping to eliminate unnecessary and time-consuming questions to staff. Improved information to consumers can also enhance the agency's public image: an opinion poll in the UK, for example, showed that consumers are more satisfied with local authorities that keep them well informed (120).

There is, of course, nothing wrong with informaton that accomplishes the goals of making life easier for the agency and enhancing the agency's PR image.

But information must directly serve consumer needs too, and not just agency needs. The information provided should not only be about procedures, opening hours, etc. It should be useful to consumers for practical problem solving. Real consumer information tells people what to expect from a service and what to ask for if they do not get it. That is much more contentious as the case of one consumer group, a Community Health Council (CHC) in the UK, has shown. The CHC prepared a guide to maternity services in the District, an inner city area of London. But problems arose when the CHC asked the health authority to make it available to women who came to use the services. Because it gave consumers information about options for medical treatment, what they could ask for and what they could refuse, the front-line staff found it unacceptable. It committed the staff to certain behaviours that they thought unfair to them. In particular the obstetricians disliked the guide. They were unhappy having consumers know information about treatment options. As the CHC director said, "Its (the guide's) finest accolade came when the compiler was told by an obstetrician, without apparent irony, that the District was going to have to produce its own guide because the CHC's was biased in favour of he patient!"(156).

Simplification

Closely related to information giving is the question of simplifying the underlying rules and procedures, so that information given out about them can be comprehensible, and so that officials can be reasonably expected to administer the service knowledgeably to the public. Rules and regulations that affect quality of life have multiplied enormously in recent decades. For example an OECD publication (114) points out that until the 1920's the annual production of laws and regulations in the UK was contained in about 125 pages; it now requires over 2,500 pages. In the UK as well as in Germany, France, Denmark and other countries, there are now efforts to simplify, or "de-bureaucratise", the administration and provision of public services. This may take any of a number of forms: removing needless steps and laws; simplifying forms; eliminating unnecessary forms; standardising procedures.

A great deal of effort is being placed on such developments in Germany. In the Lander in the late 1970's and at the federal level after 1983, officials embarked on a more radical programme of de-bureaucratisation than in any other European country, with tangible results. For example, in Bade Wurtemberg the number of official circulars was reduced from 16,000 in 1979 to 4,000 by 1984.

Similarly, the Central Forms Unit set up in the UK national government in 1982 identified 104,000 forms in use and in its first two years of operation abolished 9,400 of them.

Whether reduction of forms leads to the experience of simplification in consumers' lives is unknown. There has, however, been research on the effects of making forms simpler. Research in the UK (48) has shown that simpler, "user friendly" forms are liked by consumers and are more effective at communicating information.

However, simplification of forms necessarily depends, in great part, on simplification of the underlying rules and laws governing the services. At a recent international seminar on consumers and public services, an official of the Department of Employment in Germany said that because laws of entitlement still remain quite complex, "the questions put in the forms are difficult and can hardly be simplified"(39).

But the search for simplification is continuing in virtually all public services in most states of the

European Community. The administrative motivation is high: simplification can lead to cost savings by reducing errors and saving time. Some administrations have run huge campaigns in the search for simpler ways of doing things. For example in France a campaign in the mid 1980's called, "Faites aboutir une idée" (roughly, pull off a good idea) got 200,000 suggestions for making life simpler for consumers, including such ideas as making tax stamps available at more local sites. In Portugal, simplifying the procedure for getting tax stamps has resulted in savings to the administration of 114,000,000 Escudos per day (approximately 650,000 ECUS).

Coordination

Departmental divisions in the delivery of services to the consumer can lead to the "ping pong" administrations refered to in Chapter 2. The most usual way in which public authorities are tackling this problem is to provide a central information and referral service, often supported by a computerised database. People can phone, write or come in person and get information about the full range of an authority's services.

Thus in Spain, an interdepartmental information service received over 72,000 queries in 1986. In France, the interministerial information service CIRA (Centres Interministeriels de Renseignements Administratifs) receives over 500,000 queries per year.

Another development in coordination has been the coordination of actual service delivery, not just information about services. In central London, Westminster's One-Stop Shop is an example of this. Relying heavily on new technology, the One-Stop Shop can deliver at least the first stages of virtually the entire range of council services from one room, from getting a parking permit to registering to vote, getting social services advice and paying the rent. The room has been specially designed for pleasant appearance and an open, accessible look. Facilities include special provision for the disabled, interview rooms for confidential discussion, photocopiers, toilets, and background music. Evaluation shows that consumers who use it like the One-Stop Shop (eg "very good idea and a great improvement"; "a great improvement in environment and courtesy") (150), so much so that the authority has set up a second One-Stop Shop in another geographical area.

New technology is a key feature in many efforts to coordinate services as well as to improve services in other ways. This subject was covered in depth in an earlier RICA report for the EF (50). That report concluded that, although computers are brought in to the public sector primarily to reduce costs, consumers may nonetheless derive considerable benefit from them. The appendix of the present report provides details of how one agency (Walsall Housing Department) has tried to use technology to improve service.

New technology is being introduced in Birmingham to promote inter-agency coordination of services to mentally handicapped people. The health department and the social services department, two wholly separate agencies answering to different authorities, are coordinating their information registers on mentally handicapped clients, so that each agency may easily know what services the other agency is, or is not, providing to an individual. A report of the programme states that "... it has resulted in closer working relationships across disciplines" (21).

Coordination across different professions has chronically been difficult to achieve, though everyone agrees it is vital in order to provide effective service to the client. Various efforts are being made, some very simple but successful. For example, a health authority in Manchester has coordinated medical and chiropody services in such a way that it is the chiropodists who now dispense vitamin D to elderly women, resulting, according to the authority, in a 25 per cent reduction in broken hips.

Inter-agency cooperation in service delivery often involves having to cede a bit of authority and power, something that service providers may be unwilling to do. At another health authority in the UK, in Wales, a voluntary organisation wanted to provide a "consumer-friendly" service for elderly people being discharged from hospital. The hospital's ambulance service simply deposited people at their homes; the voluntary organisation would have delivered them and in addition helped to settle them at home. But the hospital refused to cooperate because, according to a report at a conference in Rome (135), they would be yielding budget and authority to the voluntary organisation.

Budget and authority are common stumbling blocks in coordinating services for the consumer. A project in Germany, in Dusseldorf, has set up a coordinating group of 20 local agencies to coordinate services for single parents. Professionals from these agencies meet regularly to exchange information, discuss cases and problems, invite colleagues to participate in consultations with clients and so on. Although the organisers of the project feel important gains have been made in service delivery, attendance at these coordinating meetings has suffered because work in the project is still considered by the individual institutions to be "supplementary ... priorities of work are set by the institutions, not by the project" (61). How to share out the costs is also a problem: payment to these agencies is normally based on case load, but the coordinating model involves more fluid ways of working, and counting cases is not considered fair or appropriate any longer.

Marketing approach

> *"Market research is the voice of the consumer ... It is the means by which ordinary people can influence ... goods and services and the formulation of social policy"*(102).

Many organisations are now pressing public sector agencies to adopt the classic marketing techniques used by the commercial sector, in order to better serve their public. In France, ARAP (Association pour l'Amelioration des Rapports entre l'Administration et le Public), an organisation formed in 1975 and partly funded by central government, recently called for a marketing approach in public services (4). In the UK, the LGTB (Local Government Training Board) has been very active in pressing for such an approach for several years now.

In a discussion paper published in 1985 (100), the LGTB pointed out that adopting a marketing approach is not a matter of "selling" a service or even creating a demand; since demand is usually greater than provision, marketing in the public sector is about targetting a service. It is looking at how to make effective use of often meagre resources to make sure the people you want to serve *are* served. In other words, the LGTB approach to marketing is to make practice reflect policy.

A marketing approach involves focusing attention on the consumer, answering such questions as:

☐ who are the users of the service
☐ who are the potential users
☐ how is service related to demand
☐ what do users want from a service

- what do they in fact receive
- what do potential users want
- what difficulties are encountered by people trying to use the service
- what causes those difficulties.

In the UK, one local authority, Richmond, has been commended for "the coherence and sincerity" (124) of its marketing approach. In 1986, Richmond established the post of Senior Market Research Analyst, attached to the office of the Chief Executive. Through this post, the authority hires a professional market research agency to conduct regular surveys among citizens and among consumers of the services to monitor changes in attitudes to the authority and views on its performance; to test attitudes to new policy options; and to gauge the impact of previous initiatives. All department managers must prepare annual reports stating how they have tapped the views of consumers.

Richmond has brought the marketing approach to bear on meals services for the elderly, respite care for families with disabled children, public housing services, and needs for preschool children. The authority has shown itself fully prepared to change its plans in response to market research results. For example, a planned Family Centre for under 5's, bringing together social services, education, etc. under one roof, was dropped when market research with mothers of preschool children showed a consumer preference for other solutions, e.g. more public financial support for childminders; lowering the starting age for school. A "mobile town hall", a van fully equipped with computers and trained staff to deliver virtually all council services, had its route and opening hours changed to suit consumer preferences, revealed in market research better; the change led to a 20 per cent increase in use.

Richmond is only one of many public authorities that now survey their citizens to help to plan services. For example, in the German town of Datteln, a 1987 survey led to the Social Affairs Committee making a number of changes, including extending the opening hours of day care centres from 20 to 30 hours per week and developing plans for restructuring the youth programmes "to be more user-oriented" (55). Central and local government bodies in Spain, France, Portugal and the Netherlands are also beginning to survey their consumers.

But often such moves are not taken in the context of an overall commitment to a comprehensive market approach. Consumer surveys are relatively easy to do, but they are only a means to an end; thought must be given to the much greater difficulty of incorporating the findings of consumer surveys into the planning and delivery process. Pre-1983 there were virtually no surveys of patients in the UK health service; now there are so many it is impossible to count them all, but a recent inquiry found that "it has been a rarity for any action to be taken by (service) managers as a result of their surveys of patient opinion" (90).

It is necessary to create the "organisational space" to translate the information about consumers yielded by surveys into institutional policy and practice. In other words, authorities have to make room for the market information in the decision-making process. Major organisational and cultural change is required to do this effectively, and we will deal with this later in the paper.

At this point, it is worthwhile to divert slightly to further clarify what is meant in this paper by "consumerism" in the public sector. There has long existed a movement to organise people at the local level to better express their needs as consumers of service. But consumerism in this paper is not about community self-expression. It is about the public administrative process, and about *changes in the process itself* to accommodate and institutionalise consumer influence. It is one thing for community groups to organise and to express their needs; it is quite another for civil servants to take any notice of them. This paper is about getting civil servants to notice, and to act.

Returning to consumer opinion polls we find that, widespread though they are becoming, they are still far from entirely accepted as a legitimate activity for public servants. It is still very common to hold the view expressed in one study in France that, "...officials are very close to the public and quickly come to know their dissatisfactions, without need of opinion polls" (84). But as others have put it, "...just when the staff think they know what the public want, danger starts. If one knows, one does not need to find out: a sign of the enclosed organisation" (142), i.e. the organisation that is not responsive to consumers.

Consumer surveys and market research do not supplant either the political process or professional judgement. The authority still exercises authority, but should know what consumer views are and be able to justify departing from them.

The objection is sometimes raised that a marketing approach is only appropriate for articulate consumers who have less need of help anyway. But in the UK a market research approach has been used to plan services for psychiatric hospitals (106) and for elderly sufferers of dementia (111). In the latter case, the research "highlighted the problem of interviewing sufferers of dementia ... But with adaptations to the usual interviewing technique, it was possible to achieve a number of productive interviews ... and all provided further insight into the problems, and therefore the needs of sufferers..". As Stewart and Clarke (142) have noted, the difficulty in getting consumer input lies less in *how* to do it than in *wanting* to do so.

Indeed a market research approach is not only possible, it is essential in ensuring services are used by those in greatest need: the elderly, the vulnerable, those who are less likely to come forward and claim services (51).

Some researchers (e.g. 78) advocate that to ensure disadvantaged groups have real influence in market approaches, the best way is class-weighted surveys, whereby low-income and other disadvantaged groups are over-sampled.

Before leaving the section on the marketing approach, it is worth pointing out that people like it when their views are consulted. For example a recent survey by the Consumers' Association found that 87 per cent of patients' think their doctor should try to find out patients views of the practice's services (32). It is seen as a demonstration of concern, and for that reason may be open to abuse. Opinion polling may be carried out, not as part of a commitment to a comprehensive market approach to delivering service and discovering problems, but to polish the agency's image.

Complaints procedures

Although there has been growing recognition of the value of systematically seeking information from consumers of public services, little of this recognition has been extended to one particular form of information from consumers: complaints. Complaints constitute valuable management information, but typically in the public service complaints are unwelcome and complainants are viewed as, "malcontents and misfits who have problems other than the one complained of" (99).

Studies in the UK (99, 133, 112) and in France (84) have revealed the absence of effective complaints procedures in both local and central government.

Many countries e.g. Spain, Ireland, UK, France, have

some form of Ombudsman, or Mediator, to handle consumer complaints about the public service, but these tend to be unknown to the majority of people (eg about two-thirds in France and the UK never heard of them); even when they are known they tend not to be used due to a variety of reasons: consumers' basic belief that no one will take any notice, their unwillingness to "make a fuss", their fear of retribution. Ombudsmen may be difficult to reach (in France the consumer's complaint must be sponsored by a deputy or senator), and tend not to give satisfaction from the consumer point of view - the majority of complaints are either settled in favour of the public agency or are rejected as being beyond the Ombudsman's remit.

There is now considerable support in the UK, particularly among local authorities (133), for the idea that within each authority there should be an integrated, well-publicised, formal complaints procedure that is automatically activated when a consumer expresses a complaint to a staff member. The National Consumer Council has outlined the necessary ingredients of a good complaints procedure in the context of social services: written rules and training for staff, including how to decide when a complaint is a complaint, the need for publicity and information to consumers, the need for an identifiable complaints officer to take it up the hierarchy as necessary and a special advocate for vulnerable clients, the need to keep a log, and the development of disciplinary and appeals procedures.

Maintaining a log of complaints is particularly important in planning and providing a consumer-oriented public service. It can enable accurate assessment of changing patterns of need, changes in staff levels required, poor performance in some areas, etc. It can aid rational decision-making.

But there is an important prerequisite in all of this. In order for a complaints procedure to function usefully, there needs to be a recognition, at all staff levels, of the right of consumers to complain. Complaints procedures must be accepted for what they are - devices for channelling information from consumer to administration - but as one researcher found, "it is still difficult for complaints to be seen as anything other than a nuisance"(112). In the vast majority of UK local authorities that do have complaints procedures, the procedures are only publicised to staff, not to consumers; that is because the procedures are seen "as protection for (staff)...in an increasingly critical environment", not as a means of providing responsive services to consumers (133). It comes down to the question, as the NCC put it, "How can we overcome the reluctance of professionals to change their attitudes to clients?" (112).

Complaints procedures cannot be effectively tacked on to an organisation that remains aloof or even hostile to consumers. In one UK local social security office, the following sign was put on the wall of the waiting room:

"Our aim is to improve our service. Has the service you received today been satisfactory? If you have helpful suggestions for an improvement, please ask the receptionist for an interview with Mr ..... Deputy Manager"

In six months, only two requests were received. This was a local office of an agency that has been criticised in numerous official reports (eg 9,17) for its poor level of consumer service, rude/unhelpful staff, lack of goals and direction. You can tack the sign to a wall, but you cannot successfully tack a complaints procedure on to a poor organisation.

UK surveys of local authority complaints procedures have found effective examples *only where other organisational changes in the consumer direction were taking place as well* (112,99).

We turn now to look at these much more fundamental changes in an organisation. Even more so than in the preceding six initiatives, the following initiatives are very much intertwined, although for clarity's sake we will continue to present the different emphases under separate headings.

Culture change

Over 30 years ago, Peter Drucker raised the concept of organisational culture in his classic work, "The Practice of Management", when he said that the job's objectives tell managers what they ought to do; the way a job is organised enables managers to do it; but "it is the spirit of the organisation that determines whether (they) will do it" (43).

Spirit, culture, vision, values - these are all words that are being used now in the public sector to describe an organisational commitment to consumer orientation, an attitude which is increasingly perceived by some as essential backdrop to new initiatives.

According to this view, service for the public has to be the key value for the organisation, providing motivation and purpose for the entire staff, "a shared vision" (123). Instilling this vision then becomes an important step towards creating a priority for change.

You need to get staff talking about consumer-oriented service. A standard piece of management wisdom holds that if everyone is talking about a problem, it is already on its way to a solution. In the UK, the Local Government Training Board recommends a formal launch or event to create a setting, preferably away from the office, to raise and discuss consumer ideas. Variants of such an "event" have been taking place in France, Sweden, Portugal, the UK, and elsewhere, ranging from serious discussion groups for a small number of selected staff members, to a pop extravaganza for thousands of managers complete with strobe lights and entertainers. An example of a focus on culture change, from the Netherlands, is presented in the Appendix.

Changing the culture (from traditional bureaucracy to an organisation that thinks about its customers) should be seen not as a goal, but as a method. Creating new commonly accepted values is a means to achieving real change, not the end itself. Public sector organisations are increasingly adopting slogans ("Making it happen"; "People first"), avowing goals (eg the DDASS - Direction Depatementale des Affaires Sanitaires et Sociales - in the Loire has published a "Quality Charter" about the need to provide the best, fastest service to consumers), and defining "mission statements", to demonstrate their commitment to the consumer. Some now dismiss these as mere "cant" (156) because too often mission statements, etc. are unrelated to the jobs being done. But, as the author of an influential UK study put it, "mission statements (had) always struck me as being rather like working alternatives to Christianity. Over the years, however, I have come to believe in the value of these statements, provided - and it is an essential proviso - that they are translated down the line...into specific standards capable of being monitored" (66).

Setting Standards

Public sector administrators are increasingly concerned to translate mission statements - or any form of stated desire to serve the consumer - into specific standards capable of being monitored. Frequently known as "performance indicators", such standards are being developed not merely to monitor performance, but also to set targets for performance and to measure the impact of performance.

The exercise of formalising and quantifying activities has often been carried out in order to increase efficiency and control (eg specifying the size of a social worker's case load) and in that respect is not particularly new. What is new is thinking about and experimenting with measures to define the standard of service from the consumer point of view.

This is difficult. A recent study of UK local government services in housing, day-care etc. (110), in authorities that were already disposed to "serve the customer", asked the different departments to state what standards they were aiming for. The study found that most could give none, or had only vague, non-operational notions. For example, one said "to increase the sum total of man's happiness".

Many public organisations are beginning to develop a sophisticated approach to defining consumer-oriented standards of quality of service. Particularly in the health sector in the UK, the Netherlands and elsewhere, the "Quality Assurance" approach is being borrowed from private industry whereby producers set standards for a product and its production, and take remedial action if those standards are not met.

However, it is important that there is some direct consumer input to such setting of standards. This is not always the case with Quality Assurance projects, many of whose standard-setting exercises involve only staff members. A paper at a recent international seminar in Amsterdam on consumer-oriented public service noted that public sector organisations, when they do measure performance, usually do so by their own standards rather than through the eyes of the public being served (25). This is not ideal practice, because consumer and provider views of what is good service often diverge.

For example, a series of studies of social workers in Germany (69) has illustrated the dangers of relying on asking service providers to define good quality service. There were major discrepancies between social workers and their clients in defining the standards of good service. One of the German studies asked social workers what type of help they thought people wanted, and the replies focussed on such things as sympathy, freedom to discuss personal problems etc. But the clients themselves, when asked what they wanted, focussed on practical help.

There is a need for consumer involvement in setting standards of performance. Although there are some public sector agencies that now recognise this, it must be said that most service providers probably still do not accept it. More typical are the results of a recent survey by the Consumers' Association in the UK which showed that only 16 per cent of doctors thought patients should have any role in setting good practice standards, although 87 per cent of patients thought doctors should be doing more to find out what patients think about their practice (32).

Such differences raise major issues about the role of professionalism in service provision, and this will be explored further in Chapter IV. There are many instances where the consumer view and the worker view of what is good for the consumer diverge.

Of course, even within consumer groups there are sometimes conflicting views about standards of service. In particular, those actually being served may have different views from the citizenry as a whole. That is where public services are so unlike commercial services: as Pollitt put it (122), public services generate large "externalities" that the private sector does not, in that the public sector is accountable for everyone's quality of life, not just that of the customer being served.

Nonetheless, a number of organisations (e.g. the Bloomsbury District Health Authority in London) (90) are successfully moving towards some form of consumer-defined standards. That means getting information from consumers *and* potential consumers about their felt needs and preferences, and feeding that consumer information back into the institutional decision-making process that determines the services provided. The institutional absorption of that information is the essential step in standards setting.

In Sweden, the public training agency SIPU works with

authorities to help them, as institutions, to absorb information obtained from consumers and incorporate it into the management process. They do this often by means of two-way diagrams that are constructed to elucidate differences of opinion between consumers and providers on service standards, between consumers, and providers' views of service standards. Data are fed into the following type of diagram:

	SUCCESS	
STANDARD	Low	High
Important		
Not important		

The significant finding is that concerned with standards which appear in the top left square (important, but perceived to be poorly achieved) for consumers, and which for providers. Such results are systematically fed into staff study groups to focus discussion on the conditions of good service, to stimulate the emergence of solutions and to set standards at which to aim.

This method was used in the mid-1980s by the Northern Ireland Housing Executive. It was discovered, for example, that staff underestimated the importance that consumers attach to having a good public reputation. This finding was then discussed and debated in detail in staff "Quality Service Groups" to decide what it meant and what should be done about it. In the Northern Ireland exercise it was found, in all, that there were six standards of service (out of 13) where staff and consumer views were discordant, i.e. staff and consumers differed in their views as to whether those particular standards were important indicators of performance.

In the UK, the National Consumer Council (NCC) has

recently completed a comprehensive exercise with two local authorities - in Newcastle and in Cambridgeshire - to develop a series of consumer-oriented performance indicators in housing, day care, library, refuse and street lighting services (110). The aim was to encourage all authorities to set explicit targets of performance and, importantly, to provide consumers with information that would enable them to assess public performance and thus to press for improvements where indicated.

The starting point for the NCC was to get information from consumers about their needs and preferences, to determine the standards of service that are important from the consumer point of view. The consumer information collected was both quantitative and qualitative, and sometimes relied on "proxy" indicators. That is, the NCC not only determined what parents of children under five said they wanted in the way of day care, but also estimated need by looking at proxy indicators such as number of single parent families, whether and where mothers work, indices of social stress etc.

The exercise has been quite successful in focussing local government officers' minds on the consumer, and has been taken up by the Local Government Training Board in its activities with authorities throughout the UK. Authorities are being encouraged to use consumer information to set standards, to monitor comparative performance across authorities (in Kent, councillors were shocked into action when comparative survey results told them "You are bottom of the pile" among neighbouring authorities) and to shift targets upwards as earlier consumer targets are achieved (in Portsmouth, information from housing consumers concerning helpfulness of repair staff was used to set targets of tenant satisfaction; when those target levels were met, even higher targets were set).

But the NCC also produced a series of leaflets intended for use by consumers themselves. The leaflets provide a consumer checklist that can be used by the public, not just the staff, to assess service standards.

This consumer aspect of standards setting is very important, but also very contentious. It is clear that consumers need some sort of yardstick to determine whether a service is poor. If a train does not arrive at the time published in the schedule, the consumer knows the service is poor. But if it takes six months wait to get space in a home for the elderly, is that poor? Should the consumer complain?

Without published performance standards, there is no way of knowing. These kinds of performance standards would constitute *real* consumer information - not just a list of what services exist, but also a public commitment to a particular standard of service.

Not many agencies do this. In the US, hospital-by-hospital figures were released in 1986 showing mortality rates - crude, but they generated enormous discussion of consumer issues in the media. Authorities are understandably reluctant to publicise information which bears on standards of service. As Pollitt put it, "...to ask them to volunteer highly sensitive performance information... to an unpredictable, unprofessional and highly self-interested public may appear a less than overwhelmingly attractive course of action" (122).

Decentralisation

One of the more obvious ways of "getting close to the customer" is just that: getting physically, geographically, closer to the public being served. In the UK, 61 per cent of all local authorities now have some form of decentralised system. In Spain, decentralisation began in Madrid in 1979 and is now judged to be 80 per cent complete, with 18 self-governing districts. Many French towns and cities have been decentralised, e.g. Lille started to decentralise in 1975 and, with ten neighbourhood town halls, decentralisation was complete by 1987. Decentralisation of municipal governments is also taking place in the Netherlands, in Italy, in Sweden. Decentralisation of the highly centralised national government was decreed in France in 1982. In Greece a 1985 government report called for decentralisation from central to local government (as of 1988, this had not been implemented).

These all represent vastly differing forms of decentralisation, with differing objectives, of which getting closer to the consumer to deliver faster, more responsive service may be only one. Other, related, objectives include increasing local accountability, enhancing community development, promoting equal opportunities, raising political awareness, projecting a better public relations image, improving job satisfaction. A huge body of literature is being generated about decentralisation but a recent review points out, "there has been a dearth of evaluative work on decentralisation" (154). The same review goes on, " 'It is quite enough to get decentralisation to happen without at the same time trying to crawl over everything we do to see if it's working perfectly' is an understandable response".

Getting decentralisaton to happen is difficult. In one local authority in the UK (Islington, London), after the political decision was taken to set up some decentralised services, arguments raged in headquarters over how this was to be done, what would be retained at the centre, etc. A journal article described what happened (126): 'In the midst of these disputes, fate took a hand in the form of a burst water main outside the central office in the second day of what was to be a six-week long water workers' strike - forcing the dispersal of the 200 headquarters staff to 15 day and residential units.' In a curious way the disembodied state of the department made it easier to think from first principles.

Much of the literature is preoccupied with the process and mechanics of decentralising. Nonetheless, research on impact is starting and results are emerging. This is such a large subject that it would require an in-depth review of decentralisation alone in order to deal adequately with the results. The present paper, however, is intended as a brief overview of all developments in consumerism, and so we will extract only a few major points, recognising that it is merely skimming the surface of the subject.

☐ *Decentralisation can make services more responsive, particularly in housing, but because the establishment of a local neighbourhood office raises consumer expectations of service, demands for service can rise quite dramatically and therefore response times can actually lengthen.*

☐ *People who use the decentralised offices for*

social services, housing, etc. may tend to be the most disadvantaged consumers, those with the most intractable social problems, and so overall improvement is even more difficult to detect.

☐ A network of smaller, autonomous, decentralised units can be more confusing to consumers than centralised service; in France, for example, the divisions of responsibility among newly decentralised services are reportedly not well understood and are causing confusion. In the UK, of the 61 per cent of local authorities that have some form of decentralisation most - four fifths - have decentralised only one service, which can lead to confusing fragmentation.

☐ Decentralisation of service delivery structures has often not been accompanied by decentralisation of decision-making processes, a situation which in the words of the Prime Minister of France, "doesn't make sense" (2). If decisions still have to be referred up the line to the centre, there seems less point to decentralisation. Getting geographically closer to the consumer through decentralisation does not necessarily, in practice, make services more consumer-responsive, or changed in any way at all.

☐ *Decentralisation can only succeed if it takes place in the context of changed attitudes. It can be "window dressing", mere mechanics, if it is not motivated by a genuine desire to serve the consumer better.*

Personnel Practices

The personnel an agency recruits, and how they are trained, promoted and paid, clearly play a crucial role in the kind of service the agency delivers. Public sector organisations are increasingly thinking about, and experimenting with, new personnel practices that will favour consumer-oriented service.

RECRUITMENT

Recently, a job advertisement for a post in local government appeared in a British newspaper announcing that the authority "...is customer oriented and only those prepared to dedicate themselves to the needs of clients need apply" (*Guardian* 17 June 1987). This was just one of many similarly-worded ads that have been placed by public sector agencies to recruit personnel with a view to implementing their new consumer-oriented philosophy.

A strong view is apparent in the literature, and emerged in interviews conducted for this paper, that bringing about consumer-oriented change is dependent to a large part upon the individual personality of the public servants involved - that some will readily and enthusiastically adopt a consumer orientation, that others will not, and that those who will not should be left alone, not forced to go along with change. Therefore, recruiting the right new staff becomes important in page promoting consumer service.

It is interesting that while some authorities are using recruitment to promote a consumer philosophy, others are advocating just the reverse: the use of a consumer philosophy to promote recruitment. Speaking at an international conference on consumerism, the Controller of the Audit Commission in the UK responsible for monitoring quality of service in local government argued the need for a consumer approach because, "It has become increasingly difficult to entice high quality local citizens into local government which is seen as a low status activity" (35). In France too (147,84) it has been noted that morale in public sector service is low and that this problem could be counteracted by a consumer orientation. Others too have suggested that adopting a consumer approach will counteract such morale problems, that it provides "a sense of purpose" (142) that will rejuvenate image and practice in the public sector. Independent evaluation of a consumer-oriented local government project in England (see Appendix for details of Walsall programme) provides some evidence that consumer orientation may lead to greater job satisfaction, as does a project in Sweden (see Appendix).

TRAINING

It is not possible to tell staff, "Be consumer-oriented"; they must be taught how to do the job in a manner different from that previously used. Providing consumer-oriented service requires new professional skills at all levels, not just making counter staff aware that they must speak courteously to consumers, although that is important. Staff at all levels need to acquire new skills and knowledge to serve the consumer better. For example, do staff in contact with the public know enough about all the authority's policies to be helpful to the consumer? Do they have the "people skills" of listening, helping, defusing conflict? Do they know how to write a short letter using simple words? Managers, too, need all these resources, and more: how to run or commission market research; how to manage a decentralised operation; how to set up a complaints procedure.

But commitment to in-service training in the public sector, whatever the subject, has generally been inadequate in most EC countries. In France, Paul Ripoche, director of the Association for the Improvement of Relations between the Administration and the Public, noted that "further training for civil servants is not really training at all, in the sense of developing the human capital and the creativity of the service. It takes place mainly to pass on rules and practices to staff, to guarantee the continuity, tradition and interchangeability of staff" (5). It is training as perpetuation, not training as development.

Ripoche's organisation, ARAP, as well as, for example, the Fachhochschule fur offentliche Verwaltung in Germany (North Rhine-Westphalia), SIPU in Sweden, the Royal Institute for Public Administration in the UK and others, have been offering training courses for junior staff as well as managers, to provide the skills and techniques required to operate a new kind of service to the public. Training is being viewed not only as a necessity for the service, but as an opportunity for public servants themselves who know "under their skins" (147) that their image with the public is poor and that professional training is necessary to raise their public esteem.

In Denmark, the Local Government Training Centre has developed a unique five-day video and audio training package to improve the skills and awareness of all staff who have to come in contact with the public. The package is self-operating: it requires no trainer to be present and small groups of staff (maximum size is 20) can set up their own schedule to watch it, follow the programmed breaks for group discussion, and repeat it as many times as desired for in-coming staff. Since the package was developed in 1980, two-thirds of Denmark's 275 local authorities have used it. It is offered free of charge. Feed-back received from the developers of the package, Den Kommunale Hojskole i Denmark, suggests that it has been very successful.

INCENTIVES

A number of public sector organisations are experimenting with reward schemes to reinforce consumer-oriented service. The natural resistance to change is strong and authorities in the Netherlands, the UK and elsewhere are trying to introduce incentives to overcome this resistance. The incentive schemes being tried are often modest in the extreme, i.e. small cash awards or prizes for coming up with a good consumer idea or practice; but in some cases the cash awards are large, and sometimes general up-grading in salary is negotiated to facilitate consumer-oriented service.

There is at least a potential for consumer-oriented service to be incorporated as a routine element in performance appraisal and performance-related pay schemes, but this appears to have been very little developed so far. What is worse, as a recent OECD publication (114) pointed out, is that existing performance incentive schemes may actually militate *against* good consumer service. In one public authority, an attempt to increase responsiveness to the consumer through training and by encouraging staff to take time to listen to the consumer failed, because the policy

conflicted with a performance incentive scheme based
on increased daily case through-put. Thus it is
necessary for an organisation to ensure that all its
personnel policies are consistent with consumer service.

PROMOTION
There is another, more fundamental, inconsistency in
personnel policies: those staff in direct contact with the
consumer are often at the lowest level of the
organisation, and if they are good at the
job they are promoted up, and out of
consumer contact. A number of
authorities are trying to come
to grips with this problem.
In the UK, in Walsall
Housing Department,
a new career structure
has been created for
housing officers in
decentralised
neighbourhood units,
permitting them to rise up the administrative hierarchy
while remaining in direct service to the consumer. In
Germany, in the Hamburg police department, a new
post of special foot patrol officer has been created:
those who have skills at establishing good relations with
the public can now be promoted as high as Inspector
grade while still staying on the beat. These very senior
and experienced officers are given a great deal of leeway
to use their time on the streets as they see
fit and the head of the Hamburg police force has
reported that the scheme has lead to a ''very positive
reaction of the general public (95).

Two-way Staff Communication

Staff in contact with consumers may have a more
accurate view of consumer needs and attitudes than do

middle and senior managers, but they are at the bottom of the traditional bureaucratic hierarchy and their views are neither sought nor valued. The normal flow of information is top-down, but increasingly authorities that want to provide a more consumer responsive service are recognising the need to listen to their "front line" staff, through a bottom-up flow of information.

But you cannot just "order" previously de-valued staff to participate in down-up developments. After years and years of a public service "founded and organised on the basis of a principle of mistrust" in the front line (2), it is necessary that junior staff be given training, opportunity and encouragement to voice their views. As a speaker at a conference on public sector consumerism in London put it, "The inability to listen is so often matched by an inability to talk". (6)

New procedures and structures are being introduced in Sweden, France, the UK and elsewhere specifically to encourage better two-way internal communication. Opportunities are built into the work routine for junior staff and the management to sit down together and discuss consumer service issues and problems in an open, non-threatening setting. That is the essential concept behind a number of initiatives, including Quality Circles, Service Days, Customer Care Groups, etc., now taking place in the public sector in Europe.

The Local Government Training Board in the UK has provided detailed guidelines on how to plan and run Service Days in an authority (101). They involve setting aside specific periods of time away from the office, in a relaxed environment, bringing together representatives from *all* levels ("Frontline staff are essential") with an agenda to discuss specific questions (e.g. who are our consumers, what do consumers think is good service, what are the barriers to good service). There is also an open "brainstorming" session for improving service, and a phased action plan is finally produced. It is in these contexts that consumer opinion polling results are often introduced.

It has been argued that to decentralise without instituting the structures for better two-way staff communication simply exacerbates the isolation of front line staff and hence the isolation of consumers whose only contact is with the receptionist, the case worker, the housing officer. Such front line staff must feel they can, and actually be able to communicate with senior management at the centre. The deputy director of housing in decentralised Walsall goes further in insisting that management (the "back line") see itself as working *for* the front line, rather than the other way round. The front line job, in touch with the consumer, is the important one and management should be there to support the front line. Drawing on the increased capacity for information exchange conferred by new technology, whereby the front line can get from the back line all the information it needs to serve the customer effectively, while at the same time permitting the back line to know what the front line is doing, Walsall housing department has attempted to put such ideas into practice (see case study in the Appendix).

Accountability and Autonomy

The social worker, the housing officer, and the nurse may be seen as powerful by the consumer, but such staff members often do not see themselves that way. They may feel they are — and they may in reality be —insignificant and powerless cogs in the system with no real power to influence decision-making. In the previous section we dealt with two-way communication whereby frontline and management staff are encouraged to exchange information. In this section we turn to a more radical version, and some may say a logical extension of, bottom-up communication, which is to delegate real power and responsibility to service providers in closest touch with consumers.

The idea is now being advanced by many (e.g.

142,148,72,84,77) that rules and regulations about activities that are imposed from above, and that are filtered through a multi-tiered management structure, restrict the capacity of staff to respond to consumers; that lack of discretion at the point of contact leads to a lessened capacity for service. Those at the interface who provide the service must have more power and responsibility delegated to them.

Decentralisation of the physical structures is of little use, according to this view, if those at the centre retain all control, and staff must still "answer to" the centre. Service delivery systems must be decentralised and management tiers flattened so that staff have more control over, and are accountable for, the quality of service to the consumer.

A study of the public sector in France concluded that lack of accountability itself made bottom-up movement of information impossible (84). In an experiment with Quality Circles, workers were occupied totally with satisfying their superiors and following their direction. This stifled bottom-up information flows, and was responsible for failures of Quality Circles in the French public sector. The initiative emerged as superficial, not dealing with the underlying problems of administrative organisation; ie the Quality Circles took no account of "The Pyramid".

The management consultant Charles Handy has written, "You cannot run (effective) organisations by command. For one thing, the people on the job often have more information than the would-be commander ... Organisations have to be run by ... consent ... Whereas the manager of the past ... could solve every problem, the (new) manager ... develops other people's capacity to handle it....*Everyone* has to be capable or nothing happens". (77).

This theme has been taken up and developed by Van Otter in the public sector in Sweden. It is not up to management to set rules, but rather to provide a vision or corporate culture, to delegate responsibility, and to keep control only by monitoring results, not by specifying the tasks to be done. And all this should take place in a "flatter" structure (i.e. fewer management tiers). In this way, the front line workers become participants in management. Employee responsibility is thus seen as an essential part of the strategy to improve consumer effectiveness and revitalise the public sector.

Experiments that have put such ideas into practice are being tried in a number of locations, and two are presented in the Appendix.

But increased accountability and autonomy are not being proposed only for front line staff. It is also being seen as important to promote better accountability and autonomy amongst department managers. In Canada, for example, contracts are now being, signed between the Treasury and Department of Employment managers, that increase the managers' accountability for the delivery of services. The contract specifies a series of performance results which managers must attain, but in return managers are given greater control over budgets, staff, physical planning, etc. "to give senior departmental Managers the increased authority and flexibility they need ... to manage effectively" (45). In the Netherlands some local authority department managers, for example in social services, are also signing contracts that trade autonomy for results.

It is obvious that the concept of accountability necessarily involves evaluation of some sort. Without evaluation, there can be no knowledge of results for which service providers - front line or managers - can be held accountable. The concept of accountability implies a determination to demonstrate what has or has not been achieved. The reader is referred again to the section on standards setting for a discussion of consumer-oriented performance measures.

Competition

"No provider ... should count on a guaranteed recipient for his effort" (148)

There is a growing view that an element of competition may have to be introduced into the public sector in order to encourage providers to think more about satisfying their consumers. It is significant that the quotation above comes from Sweden, long established as the classic welfare society, but where a number of commentators are now calling for such commercial concepts as competition, choice, vouchers.

Consumerism in the public sector is a relatively new development, but the idea of competition is newer yet. Increasing reference is being made to it in the literature on social services, health etc. (35,91,137,67,27,136,78) but there are as yet few instances in Europe where the ideas are actually being put into practice. In the US and Canada, voucher systems have been used for such services as day care and transport for the elderly for some time now, permitting consumers greater choice of service. For example, if vouchers are given to parents of mentally handicapped children, they can choose whatever service or combination of services that is available. And instead of having an authority decide that the parent will get an inflexible, say, weekly, day off from caring for the child, the parent can trade in the vouchers for varying services or periods, e.g. an evening off, or save up for a two week holiday. It permits consumers a bit more control over their services.

Up until recently such notions as the use of vouchers had "...for some reason become a right wing cause in Britain...a pity, since vouchers ... provide consumers with choice and dignity and producers with instant data for future planning on what services are most appreciated", according to a social services director from a London borough (136). But public thinking in such matters is changing in the UK, and in Sweden it has always been made clear that competition could and should be introduced within a public welfare model: providers should have to compete for clients in order to sustain budget and staffing, but standards would have to be introduced and monitored by government to preserve quality and equity.

In the US, the UK and elsewhere, housing is moving away from the single, monolithic public housing department, toward much more pluralistic forms of provision. At a seminar in London in 1989, "Managing the Public Services", Robin Hambleton of the School for Advanced Urban Studies, in Bristol, described alternative arrangements for housing, including housing associations, tenant management groups, tenant corporations, "and other forms we haven't even invented yet" (76).

Recent legislation in the UK has made it possible for housing tenants to choose whom they would like for a landlord. It remains somewhat of a fanciful, if intriguing, notion that a social services client who did not like one social services department could take his custom to a neighbouring one. But that is precisely what is now being advocated by some. As the Controller of the Audit Commission put it, "Competition in the public sector is one of those things that works in practice but not in theory" (36).

Consumer Participation and Representation

Innovations are being tried to enable consumers to participate directly in public sector decision-making, viewed by many as the "highest" form of consumerism

(75). In fact, some would dismiss all the previous 13 categories of innovation in this paper as mere "managerialism" believing that only full democratic participation in decision-making will make public services serve the public.

Of course, consumer representative groups have participated in decision-making in the public services for many years in the UK, France, Belgium, and elsewhere, eg CHC'S, Comites d'Usagers. But these bodies are widely criticised in the literature (eg 84,31,94,128,137,33,46) for lacking power and independence, for being "tacked on" to systems but not integrated for being given neither teeth nor resources, and for generating no great public interest. The latter problem may be a function of all the others. Public sector administrators have seen little need to work with such groups, which only serves to further weaken them.

In similar vein, authorities in most EC countries have had long-standing requirements for public consultation, particularly on planning matters, but such meetings "tend to be ritual occasions... frustrating for both sides..."(31); "a procedural hoop which needs to be jumped through and then forgotten" (101). No wonder the public are apathetic about attending.

Difficulties in getting consumers to participate in the past have led to criticisms being levelled at consumers themselves, as if there were something wrong with them. But the question of how to get consumer participation should not be seen as a shortcoming of consumers; it should be viewed rather as a problem of providers. What has been on offer may be unattractive. Systems and institutions may need to change, not consumers.

Many of the changes now being advocated, and tried, reinforce consumer participation by endowing it with real power. Consumers in the public sector are beginning to be given fiscal and legal muscle in order to redress the inherent imbalance of power between consumers and providers. This may integrate consumer influence better, and enable consumers to participate in innovative ways at the highest levels of decision-making.

Before we go on to look at some of these experiments, we would like to try to answer an objection frequently raised to the idea of consumer participation in public sector decision making: that it is unnecessary, because the democratic electoral system already gives consumers power.

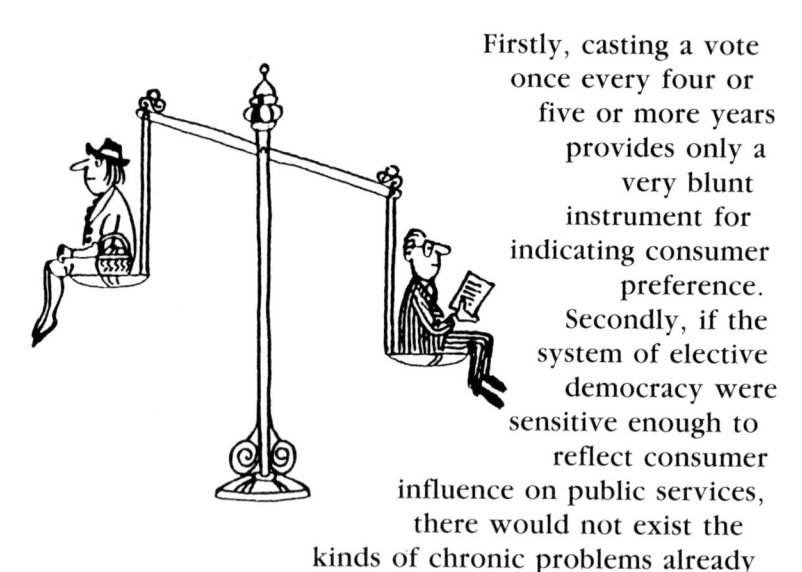

Firstly, casting a vote once every four or five or more years provides only a very blunt instrument for indicating consumer preference. Secondly, if the system of elective democracy were sensitive enough to reflect consumer influence on public services, there would not exist the kinds of chronic problems already described. Thirdly, there is plenty of precedent for extra-electoral participation in public decision-making to represent particular interests, viz., trade unions. And as to that last point, it has been claimed that trade unions represent consumer needs; we do not believe that this is the case. Worker and consumer views often diverge, as has been mentioned already and will be discussed further in section IV.

A very ambitious experiment is taking place now in London. Islington, an inner city district of London, decentralised its services into 24 neighbourhood offices beginning in 1982. Attached to each office is a Neighbourhood Forum, representing residents of the area, which has constitutionally defined powers to determine how services are provided and how money is spent in that area. As a Council report put it, "The public will be therefore involved in running services in a way normally denied to them" (86). It is up to each Forum to decide how its membership should be made up - elections, nominations, or both. Forums have the power to spend money on environmental improvements as well as for capital spending. Furthermore, the professional managers of the neighbourhood office are accountable to the Forum. A two-year research project by an external team had just begun, at time of writing, to evaluate the impact of the programme in Islington.

Although not so comprehensive in scope, a number of other authorities in the UK are also attempting to give real power to consumers through giving them spending power, e.g. Middlesborough, which has set up community councils, each with a small budget to use as it wants. Ceding spending power to consumer representatives is a significant innovation. But other ways of integrating consumer groups in the decision-making process in the public sector are also being tried. One such is the establishment of consultative groups that bring together providers and consumers in one council. By bringing the two sides together around a table, in an institutionalised, routinised way, it is hoped to avoid the isolation frequently suffered in the past by separate consultative bodies composed solely of consumer representatives, which were perhaps easier to ignore. As Richardson put it, "when consumers and decision-makers confront each other directly, they have the greatest opportunity to engage in bargaining - to persuade, cajole and win concessions - to gain, in short, some ground. In the absence of such contact, they can try to do so, but their very isolation limits their ability to do so effectively" (127).

A successful example was the consultative body that brought together social security claimants and government welfare officials from the (then) Department of Health and Social Security in Wrexham, in Wales (see Appendix).

In Sweden, a procedure known as "conditional delegation" has been introduced by law, in order to increase the influence of consumers in local government decision-making. More authority has been delegated to front line staff, but the right to make a decision concerning certain services is delegated to employees conditionally upon their consulting with the consumers affected, before making the decision. The conditions for delegation may be limited to the requirement that there shall be non-binding consultation with the consumers, but it may be given greater weight by requiring agreement between employees and consumers.

The relevant law was passed in 1988, and it was a recognition that consultation procedures in the past were weak, and that there needed to be clearer, more genuine consumer influence.

Another new way of promoting consumer participation in decision-making has been the practice of drawing up a contract of services agreed between providers - usually social workers - and consumers which, while not legally binding, is held by some (138) to redress the imbalance of power between the two. Such contracts define the obligations of the individual worker and of the employing organisation toward the consumer, and may set goals and time scales. They also define obligations for consumers.

The great difficulty with all these forms of consumer participation is that some consumers are simply too weak or vulnerable to participate. The answer, in the UK, Sweden and the US, is advocacy. Even the most profoundly handicapped people can participate; the advocacy system is being used successfully to help all sorts of disadvantaged consumers, not only the disabled.

Advocates are people who are hired, or who volunteer, to work within the system, be it hospital, social security, or whatever, to help and support individuals in their negotiations with the authority. It is very direct and very personal, and it serves to redress, if only a bit, the power between the weaker consumer and the stronger provider. Patient Advocates with specific responsibility for Afro-Caribbean patients have been employed at a health authority in the UK since the mid 1980's. A recent study (156) was able to document improvements in health indices and reductions in complaints as a result of the advocacy project.

In the US, 75 per cent of acute hospitals now employ patient representatives because, in what is a largely commercial sector, they "improve the hospital's image" (24). It is an interesting sidelight to note that in one - public sector - hospital scheme in the UK, people hired by the local consumer health council to mediate for non-English speaking patients were actively rejected by staff. "There were times when staff seemed to prefer to use the cleaner to interpret rather than call one of the (project) workers" (24).

Advocates work in an essentially one-to-one relationship with each individual consumer to represent and promote their interests as individuals as best they can. But in a much more corporate approach, Camberwell Heath Authority was the first in the UK to employ a consumer representative to sit on the authority's management board. A new position, Head of Consumer Services, was created in 1986, and the job description called for the post holder to represent the consumer in all corporate decision-making, contribute to the corporate planning process, develop standards implement a Quality Assurance programme and formulate a complaints procedure.

Since 1984, a number of other health authorities in the UK have created a post to represent consumers atmanagement level, or more usually have simply added "consumer" to the list of responsibilities of existing managers, particularly directors of nursing. However, the potential for conflict of interest in such a situation is unfortunate - many practices have been identified which take place for the convenience of nursing staff but are not in the interests of consumers, e.g. set times for getting up and going to bed, set visiting hours - and someone whose responsibility covers both nursing and consumers may not be in the best position to resolve such conflicts.

Recently the UK journal *Public Administration* devoted an entire issue to consumerism (123). It concluded that consumerism cannot be a "bolt-on extra" to be affixed while everything else goes on as before. The Local Government Training Board has pointed out (102) that no one method will do - that a comprehensive multi-faceted strategy for change is needed. The Institut Français des Sciences Administratives has concluded that isolated piecemeal measures fail to attack the causes of dysfunction, thus ensuring that difficulties will reappear in other forms.

There is a consensus among those concerned to bring about consumer-oriented service that change has to permeate every level within an authority. The OECD, which has an on-going programme looking into relations between public administrations and their clients, asked, "Who is responsible for responsiveness?" and the answer was: everyone involved in the administration (114).

The London Borough of Richmond, which recently won an award (RIPA/Hay award, 1987) for consumer-oriented management initiatives, is active on several fronts: market research, complaints monitoring, staff involvement, consumer consultation groups, and corporate information strategy.

In Italy the City of Modena instituted a wide range of changes, including lifting the anonymity of staff, better signs in the town hall, a local Ombudsman-type of service, regular testing of consumer opinion.

A White Paper that looked at public service renewal in Ireland in 1986 called for a range of personnel initiatives such as merit pay, consumer relations training, performance appraisal with an emphasis on results, not tasks, and other initiatives, including removal of physical barriers to consumers (hatches etc.), improving the physical appearance of reception areas, creating a consumer services manager post, an element of budgetary autonomy for local managers, opening hours to suit the consumer, and regular monitoring.

Similar holistic approaches have been called for in other countries, including France and Germany. In sum, there is widespread agreement that for public sector services to change from traditional bureaucracies to organisations that serve the public it is necessary to take a "whole organisation" approach, looking at consumers, staff and management practices.

PART FOUR

Discussion

Implications for workers

The consumer initiatives described in Section III have major implications - both positive and negative - for working life. It has to be acknowledged that there has been some opposition from trade unions and professional associations, in response to the negative implications, as the literature repeatedly documents, although information has been available mainly from the UK (84,156,102,49,92,139,79,145) e.g.:

☐ *a scheme to provide individual UK civil servants with £1,000 cash bonuses for boosting departmental performance and image was described by the trade union as "an outrageous slap in the face" for staff who worked as a team (18)*

☐ *in France, in the city of Reims, the administration wanted to survey consumers on their views of the service, but the questionnaires were never distributed because the unions objected; they feared the survey would identify disagreeable staff members. In the UK, the BMA (the doctors' union) rejected government proposals for "minor" improvements in patient complaints procedures, e.g. extending the time limit from eight to 13 weeks, because it "...would be a profound change that is unacceptable..." (145)*

☐ *a survey of UK public sector consumers' schemes conducted by the Community Projects Foundation concluded, "...there is growing evidence of union opposition to, or at least suspicion of, initiatives... such as decentralisation, more locally-accountable maintenance systems, and the reorganisation of offices to remove physical barriers between staff and public" (31).*

As the Kings Fund, a health research organisation based in London, has pointed out, "...serious conflicts of interest exist between service users and service providers" (92). Conflicts of interest inevitably occur when consumers and workers must share the same space, time and resources. Consumers have priorities. But to say that service providers interpret consumer needs in ways which reflect other priorities "...is not a criticism of workers; it is an observation on the reality of their working lives".

What then are the difficulties for workers in consumer-oriented initiatives?

Consumer initiatives can mean, quite simply, more work. In a study of the health services (128), for example, staff nurses viewed a range of activities, from setting up a patient information video in the waiting room, to attending meetings of Patient Participation Groups, as an "extra" duty.

Working hours can change: counter clerks gave up the two and a half hour noon shut-down in certain French prefectures so as to provide a service when most consumers could use it; British judges have been asked to surrender part of their long holiday break, in a recent UK Civil Justice review, and to sit two evenings a week, to suit consumer needs better.

The use of consumer-based performance indicators can be, or can seem to be, threatening, particularly if such figures are made public. For example, recent suggestions in the UK that information be regularly published on pupil achievements, to enable consumers to choose among schools, have been described by teachers' unions as "crude and offensive" (113). If the quality of service is to be judged by consumer norms, it means inevitably that professionals will have to yield some of their "professionalism".

Decentralisation is particularly fraught. It can require a whole new style of working, new conditions, new colleagues, new job functions, creating problems for workers. In Stockport, in the UK, a researcher has described the "real grief" (73) felt by social workers at the break-up of old teams necessitated by decentralisation. In the Islington decentralisation scheme, social workers, housing specialists and environmental health officers working in the new neighbourhood units were expected to deal with anyone who came in "off the street", whatever their problem; the consumer goal was to provide a no-wait, accessible, coordinated service, but staff worried that this would lead to a "dilution of professional skills" (79).

The worker reaction to decentralisation in Islington has been studied in some detail, and illustrates a great many other worker concerns. There was a fear of being isolated in the neighbourhood office. The various professionals represented in each unit (social work, housing etc.) blocked a plan to appoint a supervisor in each office who would straddle departments and coordinate services, because each professional felt it was fairer to be supervised by their own heads who understood their professional subject, in central headquarters. Staff were opposed to being made accountable to the local Residents' Forum, because they worried about consumers "pursuing vendettas" against staff.

Getting close to the consumer can be threatening and painful. When a senior manager in a UK health authority sat in on discussions with consumers about services provided to people who care for the disabled at home, he was forced to confront new realities: "I heard about our services from these carers in terms that never survive transmission up the hierarchy" (89). New forms of relationships with consumers can be difficult to accept, particularly if staff have not been accustomed to treating consumers as equals. Many other problems have been raised by workers with regard to consumer-oriented initiatives: open plan offices, the removal of hatches, etc., can lead to fears of assaults on staff; complaints procedures can lead to concern over victimisation; flatter management structures, which eliminate many middle management tiers, can lead to fewer promotion opportunities; greater authority for the front line means that people higher up have to yield some of their authority; greater authority, itself, with its attendant accountability, is sometimes not welcomed by the front line - as a study in France put it, lack of accountability has, at least in the past, been felt by the unions to be a "victory" (84) in terms of job protection.

But it would be unfair and totally misleading to suggest that in every instance workers have opposed consumerism in the public sector. Workers have responded enthusiastically in some cases, particularly when attention has been paid to changing the culture of organisations, as in the Groningen example in the Appendix. Official trade union attitudes are changing too, e.g. in the UK the head of the UCW (communications workers) has agreed that "consumers ... should have direct channels into the decision making structures of public enterprises" (139); in France, public sector unions (FGAF, SNUI) have been turning their attention to serving the consumer (58).

In fact, increasingly consumerism is coming to be viewed as the instrument by which public sector employees can gain greater public respect and esteem, a sense of purpose, job enrichment and job satisfaction:

- *in Sweden, employees are getting new guarantees of job protection, training and promotion opportunities to go along with consumer initiatives.*

- *in the UK, the Local Government Training Board has, through its experience with dozens of local authorities that have introduced consumer initiatives, identified many worker benefits including, very importantly, that when customers are more satisfied, the workplace becomes a nicer, less stressful place in which to work.*

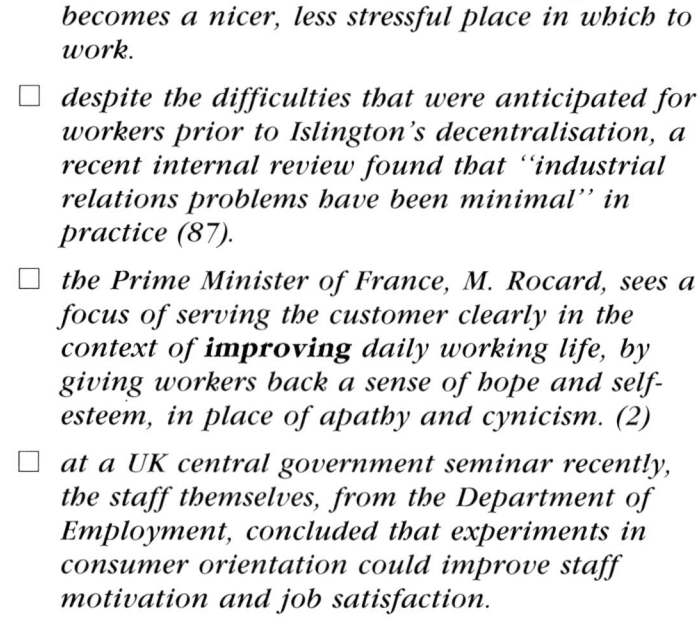

☐ *despite the difficulties that were anticipated for workers prior to Islington's decentralisation, a recent internal review found that "industrial relations problems have been minimal" in practice (87).*

☐ *the Prime Minister of France, M. Rocard, sees a focus of serving the customer clearly in the context of **improving** daily working life, by giving workers back a sense of hope and self-esteem, in place of apathy and cynicism. (2)*

☐ *at a UK central government seminar recently, the staff themselves, from the Department of Employment, concluded that experiments in consumer orientation could improve staff motivation and job satisfaction.*

The key to whether consumerism is seen as a promise or a threat may lie in effective staff consultation. Over and over again, those with experience of introducing consumer-oriented initiatives have stressed the importance of working in real and close partnership with trade unions and professional associations (eg 89,73). New policies and procedures must be negotiated carefully with staff so that greater frontline accountability does not mean scape-goating; so that formal complaints procedures serve to protect, not victimise staff; so that consumer-derived performance standards are seen by staff to be reasonable, even valuable.

But we must stress that consultation has to be real. In the consultation that preceded Stockport's decentralisation, staff felt unable to say to the management, "I think you've got it wrong" about any particular aspect of restructuring; according to one post-decentralisation analysis: "Most staff did not feel they had really participated in a consultation process at all" (73).

But even with consultation, a fundamental problem remains. We are still left with the need to resolve the inherent conflict of interest between consumers and workers. At this point it may be useful to quote from a recent publication of the Fabian Society, an organisation that has existed to promote socialism for over 100 years:

> *"...Consumerist ambitions do not always sit easily with the interests of all sections of the labour movement; in certain circumstances indeed they may be in open conflict ...*
>
> *"...The unions' raison d'etre is the advancement of their members' interests at the point of production...*
>
> *"But there is public dissatisfaction with ... the bureaucratic unresponsiveness of large parts of the public sector...*
>
> *"...The balance of forces between producers and consumers is in need of correction... We suffer from producerism: the custom of planning economic, industrial and social strategy in exclusive accordance with the wishes and convenience of producers"* (139).

It comes down to finding the right balance of power between producers and consumers of public services. The initiatives outlined in Section III of this paper would modestly empower consumers and make the relationship somewhat more equal. Providing user information, employing professionals to represent consumer interests, training staff to speak courteously to consumers, conducting performance audits based on consumer needs, instituting accessible complaints procedures, giving workers greater accountability, etc. - all these would serve to shift the balance of power slightly between providers and consumers.

It must be stressed that when we say providers, we do not mean only frontline workers. We are referring to the two sides of industry, both workers and managers, the whole arrangement of decision-making that governs consumer-provider relations; that determines, for example, that most public housing tenancy agreements in the UK place not a single obligation on the provider, but impose a long list of often ludicrous obligations on consumers (such as a rule that bathtubs must only be used as bathtubs); or that determines that dentists who leave a group practice in the UK are forbidden to tell their patient list where they are going, presumably because of resistance to the notion of competition and choice for consumers in public sector provision. The process of policy-making that arrives at this type of rule needs to be more weighted toward consumer interests, and less weighted toward provider interests. It does not deny the need for worker rights; it is a matter of finding the right balance of power between providers and consumers.

The question of provider/consumer power places the issue of consumerism firmly in the realm of politics.

The political context

There is little to be said, under this heading, than to point out the inescapable fact that consumer-oriented initiatives require political support. There will always be competing social values that are difficult to resolve, not only between consumers and providers, but also among different consumer groups, and between those who consume services and the citizenry as a whole who are not (at least at any given moment) consumers. As Klein has said, speaking about the health service, "...There may be good reasons for refusing to respond to patient preferences if meeting these reduces the overall capacity of the service to meet the needs of the community as a whole. The real difficulty is to know when this argument is being invoked because of...(provider) self interest and when it is a genuine reason for refusing to meet consumer preferences" (94). It is up to the political leaders, in a democratic society, to supply the impetus and legitimacy to consider the consumer in all such deliberations.

This political framework can be institutionalised, as in the Citizen Budget Commission in New York City, or the one being planned for Amsterdam, to represent consumers of local government services and set quality standards for government. In Britain, the Labour party has proposed a similar consumer commission which would be empowered to support consumers at the political level; and the Consumers' Association in the UK has urged consumer participation to ensure consideration of consumer interests in all decisions taken to promote the internal market of 1992.

Competing vested interests remain, but whatever the difficulty of resolving them, no progress can be made without the political will to do so. The degree of freedom service providers have in providing a consumer oriented service is defined by the political framework within which they have to work.

The real problem is lack of resources
The criticism has sometimes been made that consumerism is simply a case of rearranging the deck chairs on the Titanic. Can we "talk the language of consumerism without tackling the central realities" (67) - lack of housing, low levels of benefit payments, insufficient staff?

The answer is yes. The level at which resources are set, and that is essentially a political decision, is certainly crucial to the quality of living and working conditions, but within that level decisions must still be made as to how those resources are to be distributed. Resources will probably always be scarce. In fact, if there were enough for everybody, decision-making would be arguably *less* important. The scarcer the resources, the more important the decisions.

A Key Issue Paper published in 1989 (151) in relation to the on-going evaluation of the European Poverty Programme, covering 90 projects throughout the Community, identified four institutional factors in combatting poverty, only one of which is low levels of welfare payments. The others all fall within the framework of consumerism: the way welfare recipients are treated by the system, inflexibility of systems, and personal relations between staff and clients.

We do not wish to minimise the severe problems created by underfunding. But the fact that most European governments are now concerned to rationalise spending serves to reinforce, not weaken, the case for consumerism. If services have to be rationed, it is not logical for only the providers to settle the question of who rations them. The decision-making process should be responsive to all those affected by the decisions, including the consumer.

Consumerism and costs

Of course, getting consumer influence does, itself, cost money in terms of staff time, training, equipment, etc. That is the reason why consumer plans often either do not get translated into action, or are so under-resourced that they can have little possibility of making an impact. It may be fair to say that there is a great deal more talk than funds being devoted to public sector consumerism.

Possibly a case could be made for the cost effectiveness of consumer initiatives. There is some very limited evidence that consumer initiatives can lead to fewer complaints, more stream-lined methods,
more correctly filled-in forms, all of which can save money; in one case, a tax department, there has been evidence that a consumerist approach led to more voluntary compliance and therefore increased revenue. But very little research has been addressed to the issue of cost benefits.

It is important to note, though, that amongst those authorities that are implementing or promoting consumer initiatives, there are some that justify the idea by citing the need to remain efficient and competitive on the international front. Within the European Community, discussions are focussing increasingly on 1992 and the internal market, and in that context some officials view public sector renewal as essential for the national economy. During a 1988 meeting that was intended to enthuse managers in the French civil service on the idea of viewing the public as consumers, a government minister told them "The administration cannot remain aloof from the search for increased competitiveness in the French economy as a whole" (107).

It seems a perfectly reasonable proposition that effectiveness and efficiency in an administration go hand in hand. If public money is being wasted, consumer welfare suffers. At an earlier meeting in France in 1987, this one organised by ARAP, the group devoted to improving relations between consumers and the public sector, the chairman opened proceedings by saying that the prosperity of the country as a whole will depend on the "service imperative" in the public sector, that 1992 is not just an opportunity for private entrepreneurs; "Nations must be prepared with a modern, responsive, skilled public sector to provide the backbone of support needed ... Quality and effectiveness in the administration are coming to appear more and more clearly as one of the parameters in competitiveness" (3).

But it is indicative of other, perhaps conflicting motives, that later in the 1988 speech referred to above the minister went on to cite, as a further reason for change, the need "...to reduce the costs and expenditure connected with public administration, which represents 40 per cent of the State's expenses..." (107).

As others (153) have pointed out, consumer orientation, like any concept, is capable of distortion or misuse. It can be used as an excuse for cost cutting; it can be used to tell the client what the system is without changing it; it can be used to lull the client into accepting the level or nature of service no matter how inadequate; it can be used to buy a quiet life, to satisfy the demanding influential critics and ignore the disadvantaged consumers, the poor and the weak.

Consumerism only for some consumers?

It is certainly the case that some consumer initiatives in the public sector are directed toward privileged consumers because of the advantages for authorities - mainly financial, but also political. A study in France (84) claimed that consumer-oriented initiatives are introduced mainly in those public agencies where the customers have the equivalent of real buying power, such as in the post office, where managers have been very keen to satisfy their big business customers, mail order firms and the like. Consumer evaluation of services, opinion polls etc, are most advanced in France, according to this view, in the PTT and in the tax department, where the benefits to government are clearer than in, say, doing an opinion poll of welfare consumers. In one prefecture in France, the long noon shut-down has been eliminated for all consumer services - e.g. to get a drivers licence, identity cards, etc - except for immigration: migrants, mainly ethnic minorities, are still inconvenienced by the two and a half hour closure at noon. According to one critic, many of the new consumer initiatives "simply reproduce social inequalities based largely on income" (84).

Similar criticisms have been voiced in other EEC countries. The fear is that some consumer-oriented initiatives are only being introduced to raise the approval rating of government by the middle-class users of, for example, leisure services.

But it is nevertheless clear from the present review that a very great deal of the European activity is in fact taking place in agencies that serve a disadvantaged clientele - social services, public housing departments, services for people who are ill. And many consumer programmes originate in central government agencies whose remit is to promote good administrative practice in all government departments.

PART FIVE

Summary and Conclusions

The past decade has seen a wave of interest in consumerism in the public services - that is, in adopting a consumer-oriented philosophy of administration to *serve* the public, and in introducing various practical arrangements which will make services more responsive to consumers. This paper has outlined 14 categories of developments now taking place in some public administrations in Europe, at central and at local government level:

- **Reception** - improving the conditions of direct consumer/provider contact

- **Information** - improving the availability and nature of information for consumers about public services

- **Simplification** - reducing complexities related to rules and official forms

- **Coordination** - cutting across administrative divisions to promote coordinated delivery of different services to consumers

- **Marketing approach** - conducting surveys of consumers to find out their needs and preferences

- **Complaints procedures** - setting up agreed and publicised mechanisms for providing consumer redress

- **Culture change** - ensuring that there is a commitment throughout the organisation to consumer values

- **Setting standards** - translating consumer values into quantifiable measures and targets

- **Decentralisation** - breaking down large, centralised services into smaller more accessible units, to be closer to consumers

- **Personnel practices** - introducing recruitment, training and incentive schemes specifically to promote consumer-responsive service

- **Two-way staff communication** - encouraging front line staff, with closest knowledge of the consumer, to communicate more effectively "up the line" to management

- **Accountability and autonomy** - giving staff in closest contact with the consumer greater influence in decision-making

- **Competition** - enabling consumers to exercise some choice in the services they receive

- **Consumer participation and representation** - involving consumers directly in decisions made that affect them.

A variety of approaches is being taken. Such a variety is what is needed, and changes must permeate every level of an organisation.

Change will have important implications not only for consumers but also for providers - the workers and managers in public sector agencies. Improved service for consumers can result in greater job satisfaction for staff, and many of the consumer developments have been welcomed by staff. But some of the changed working conditions have given cause for concern. Therefore, any consumer-oriented initiatives must be introduced in close consultation with trade unions and staff associations.

Consumerism is a new development in the public sector, and there is as yet very little research in this area. In the course of conducting this project, RICA contacted over one hundred public sector and academic organisations in the European Community; only a few were able to provide hard evaluation data on the many consumer initiatives that were taking place in their countries.

Administration is a complicated business. It is rarely possible, and never cheap, to trace how a consumer orientation has influenced services. The links may in fact be tenuous, and the administrators who are introducing measures to permit and reflect greater consumer influence over decision-making are frequently acting out of an ideological commitment to consumer primacy and democratic accountability.

But the issues are far from being entirely unresearchable. Consumerism is happening, and there is a need for much more systematic research to try to clarify the status and impact of consumer initiatives.

In order to evaluate the impact of consumerism on the quality of services, much more work is needed on methods of assessing service quality from the consumer point of view. A number of organisations in the European Community have conducted some very interesting experimental work with consumer-oriented audits of service, but this needs to be developed further and applied in a variety of circumstances. Too often, even amongst administrations that think they are adopting a consumer orientation, quality of service to the consumer is measured solely according to the organisation's own standards, without any input from the consumer.

Further research is needed to assess the impact of various consumer initiatives on the quality of life of the consumers themselves. Scattered throughout this paper, and particularly in the Appendix, there are various bits of evidence that consumer initiatives work, e.g.:

- refurbishing public offices led to a reduction in environmental defacement

- the wearing of staff name badges led to reduced client anxiety

- employing consumer representatives in the health service led to an improvement in consumer health indices

- a consultative committee that brought together consumers and providers of social security services led to more than a dozen specific service improvements for consumers

- changing the culture of a social services

department, away from bureaucracy and towards consumer responsiveness, led to the department's national ranking on various criteria rising dramatically

- putting new technology directly in the control of consumers led to consumers receiving new cash entitlements
- giving autonomy to front line social workers led to a greater sense of well-being on the part of their clients.

But much more comprehensive work remains to be done to assess the effects that various consumer initiatives actually have on consumers' lives. Each of the 14 categories of initiatives in this paper could easily constitute the focus of separate study, either for a more in-depth review of existing work or, more usefully perhaps, to generate new research findings.

Similarly, the present paper provides hints, but certainly insufficient information, on the impact of consumer initiatives on the quality of working life for those who provide the services. The report has provided suggestions of both positive and negative consequences for workers, but much more systematic research is needed on this important issue.

And, finally, consumerism is taking place in the context of broader social change and other public service trends. In order to inform the debate about consumerism, it would be useful to examine consumerism in the context of other change. In particular, it would be especially useful to look at consumerism more closely in the context of the search for greater efficiency, which is characterising public administrations everywhere. Such an examination would benefit from a cross-cultural perspective, comparing the approaches to consumerism in different member states with different economies.

Among other developments, there are major changes in

demography, new technology, environmental concern, new forms of work etc; all of these may constitute both competing and complementary influences in public services. As stated in the Introduction, this paper was not intended to analyse consumerism in depth, and many provocative questions remain to be explored concerning how consumerism affects and is affected by these other social changes, e.g.: how will automation affect accountability; how will the disappearance of traditional work/leisure patterns affect consumer participation; how will conservation affect consumer choice; how will the ageing of the population - both consumers and workers - affect the developments described in this paper? Consumerism is not taking place in a void and, although this paper has focussed on consumer developments, it would be also useful to examine particular initiatives in relation to other factors of social change.

There is no single definitive formula for improving public sector services, no perfect solution. We present consumerism as an advance in the right direction. Public services exist to serve the public, and the consumer-oriented initiatives in this paper represent a way of fulfilling that simple proposition.

APPENDIX

Case Studies

Walsall Housing Service

In the early 1980's the City of Walsall, in England, decentralised its housing department into 32 neighbourhood offices, in order to bring the service closer to the consumer and to increase consumer involvement in service delivery.

The Walsall programme reflected a great many of the individual initiatives described in the present paper. For example, reception was improved by the use of open plan offices, with no physical barriers between staff and consumers. Opening hours were adapted to consumer needs by staying open Saturday morning and one evening per week. Front line staff were trained to deliver all the housing services: consumers could thus see any staff member on any issue and not be passed on to someone else. Services were coordinated not only across housing concerns (repairs, rebates etc.); the neighbourhood office was a point of contact for virtually every local government department and in some instances extended to other government agencies as well.

An independent evaluation (Mainwaring) showed that there were clear qualitative gains: consumers liked the friendly personal service, so much so that when a change in political party control of the city resulted in some closures of local units and threatened closure of others, popular demand reversed the decision. Staff, too, liked the decentralised units: they reported greater job satisfaction and even though there was a very large volume of work in the local offices, the atmosphere remained relaxed and staff morale was high.

But there were few *quantitative* gains in service to be documented. The service, "...has not altered significantly in the last five years" (7) - a statement that was made in the context of the failure of information technology in Walsall to live up to its potential.

Information technology was to have had a particularly important role in Walsall's decentralisation. There had been a conscious acknowledgement that information is indeed power. Computers were to be used to give information to consumers in ways that would redress the imbalance of power between the providers and the consumers of public services. The front line staff were to be integral to this process.

The front line staff in the neighbourhood offices were to have autonomy and, through IT, have ready access to all the information necessary to deal with consumers' needs at the neighbourhood level, without having to refer decisions "up the line". The information would be shared fully with consumers so they could understand and participate in decision-making.

But, up to 1987, it never really happened. Information and decision-making were retained too much at the centre. Front line staff were not furnished with the sort of technology that would have given them what they needed to keep consumers, and themselves, fully informed, and central computing staff were unwilling to develop the technologies required to facilitate front line autonomy. There were many specific problems e.g.: screen information and print-outs (letters, forms) remained jargon-laden and difficult to comprehend; batch processing meant that accurate information was not always available; some services were never computerised at all; others were, but shared interdepartmental databases were never made available, so the advantages of IT remained out of reach for the decentralised units.

Consumers were pleased that they had a friendly service from familiar faces. But the tremendous potential of IT remained largely undeveloped. Front line staff in the decentralised units could see what the problems were but had neither the clout nor the confidence to influence computing managers at the centre. In Walsall, "...there has been decentralisation without devolution" (7). The technological improvements that would have served the consumer, and that front line staff were aware of, were in the end simply not given a high enough priority.

Portugal Secretariat for Administrative Modernisation

In 1986, a special new unit was created in Portugal's central government, the Secretariado para a Modernizacao Administrative (SMA) - with the aim of bringing the administration closer to consumers of public services.

One of the first steps taken by SMA was to commission a market research firm to conduct a national survey of consumer views about public services, their use and experience of various departments, problems they had, and their perception of their own needs. The survey covered central and local services and included health, social services, education, the courts, social security and others.

The survey highlighted a range of difficulties in the relationship between the public sector and the consumers it is intended to serve. Findings included the facts that: consumers lacked information about public services; procedures were overly complex; behaviour and manner of civil servants towards the public were negative; the image of the public service was poor.

SMA, with a staff of only eight, launched an ambitious programme to remedy such problems. The scale of the problem was known to be quite severe even before the survey was carried out. Most civil servants in Portugal could not themselves identify the name of the ministry to which they belong, according to SMA staff, so it was not surprising that members of the public were uninformed about services. As to complexity of procedures, that too was apparent from observation: the application forms to get a passport were so complicated that law students typically gathered around the entrance to the passport office to offer (for a fee) help in filling out the forms.

The consumer poll served an important purpose in SMA's programme. In part, it established a base for monitoring progress - the poll was repeated in 1988 - and, perhaps more importantly, it served to make clear to all senior administrators the need for change. SMA launched their programme with a major conference in Lisbon to which senior civil servants were invited. The conference was called, "The public and public services: a new relationship", and during the conference the case for change was put to the 250 participants. Significantly, to demonstrate that the programme had political support, the conference was addressed by the Portuguese Prime Minister.

Since then, SMA has been working with individual ministries to promote change. SMA has an advisory capacity only - it cannot force change - but it has been given a modest budget to distribute special grants to agencies to support consumer-oriented initiatives: simplification of rules, staff training in customer relations, etc.

SMA has also launched a massive publicity campaign - leaflets, posters, booklets with new ideas, examples of good practice - both to encourage civil servants towards change, and to encourage the public to expect and demand change. It is a telling sidelight to note that one campaign poster on the theme "the public should expect the best service from us", was distributed in two versions: one in plain Portuguese, so consumers could understand it; the other in bureaucratese, so the civil servants could understand it.

Wrexham Social Security Consumer Consultative Committee

In 1986, a consultative committee of claimants and representatives of local organisations that help claimants was set up in the town of Wrexham in Wales, UK, to represent the views of consumers of government social security services in the area. The committee was organised by the Welsh Consumer Council (WCC) with the cooperation and official backing of the Department of Health and Social Security (now called the Department of Social Security).

The aims of the Committee were to ensure that the social security office was welcoming and easy to use and that it offered a high standard of service to consumers.

The Committee had some dozen local groups represented on it, plus three people who were actually consumers of social security services themselves. The consumers were recruited through newspaper advertisements and although the WCC had some initial difficulty in filling the consumer places, three suitable applicants were recruited - people who received more than half their income in state benefits and who lived locally. The Committee met regularly, about once every six weeks, throughout the first year, 1986-87.

A very important feature was that a representative of senior management of the Department of Health and Social Security attended every meeting: to answer questions, give information, report the Department's reaction to suggestions.

Because of the official liaison established with the Department, the Committee was successful in seeing a great many of its recommendations taken up by the management. In the first few months, the Committee focussed on straightforward, practical issues, like making the waiting rooms more pleasant by adding plants and pictures. But as it gained confidence as a group, it began to move toward more sensitive and complex issues, like looking at the staff/claimant relationship and the degree to which staff imparted (or failed to impart) information orally to claimants.

The management of the social security office gave recognition to the consumer committee and was from the start willing to participate in the experiment. This element of administrative involvement differentiated the Committee from the more usual form of community development group. The presence of the Administration's representative at every meeting enabled the Committee to have a routine, institutionalised path to decision-making. Although the Committee itself had no decision-making power, the arrangement was such as to permit it to successfully influence, advise and communicate with the Administration.

An end-of-year report was able to document a wide range of consumer-oriented changes achieved by the Committee, including the introduction of private interview rooms, a fast-flow system for enquiries, better signposting, a room for nursing mothers, better procedures for paying one-off benefits. More complicated issues actively under discussion at the end of the first year included training for staff, the role of visiting officers, the problems created for consumers when the Department uses temporary staff, racial discrimination, use of prepaid envelopes. These are all difficult issues, but it represents highly significant progress that consumers and staff are discussing them together.

Both the WCC and the Department viewed the Wrexham project as successful, so successful that it has recently been extended to three more locations, two in Wales and one in England (in Liverpool). The Liverpool organisers, it should be noted, have decided to allot the majority of Committee places to claimants, rather than to groups that help claimants. All three new projects will be subject to careful research evaluation, paid for by the Department and carried out by an external academic team; the results will not be available until late 1990.

Groningen Culture Change Project

Groningen is a city of 168,000 people in the north of the Netherlands. In 1987, the municipal government of Groningen launched VONK: the letters stand for the Dutch words for responsible, enterprising and client-oriented and together the acronym is Dutch for "spark".

The year before (in 1986) the local authority had completed a restructuring exercise in city government, cutting down 30 departments to 13, which made consumer service delivery more coordinated, halved the number of official forms, and reduced administrative processing time. But that was found not to be enough; it was felt necessary to change the culture, as well as the operation, of the organisation.

The VONK project had an opening day launch at Groningen's town theatre. Several hundred senior and middle managers heard what VONK was all about: improving the quality of service, stimulating employee involvement and reponsibility, and promoting consumer orientation. And a well-known entertainer composed and sang a song for them about culture change.

In those departments that responded - and none were forced to - small groups of five or six staff members were formed (VONK teams) to take the ideas forward within their own service, in a bottom-up approach. With the help of an outside management consultant group, the VONK teams developed specific plans, underwent weekend training sessions, prepared new materials, and learned how to train others so that when the management consultant firm departed at the end of their two-year contract, VONK would go on.

There was a great deal of enthusiam and activity generated - that opening day was followed by about 140 further VONK presentations to small and large groups, 250 training courses, plus contests and prizes.

Massive media publicity ensured high public awareness of VONK, all part of the near-evangelical strategy employed by the management consultants. As described in one internal report, to change the culture of an organisation it is necessary "to get a certain escape speed, to draw attention, to make the whole organisation a hive of activity... to smother the existing culture" (68).

One of the departments that did take up the VONK project was Social Services. They adopted the slogan "Kwaliteit als mentaliteit" (roughly translated: think quality); conducted market research in which they asked consumers to rate, on a scale of one to 10, their experience with the department along various criteria; distributed the survey results to all staff; and asked for staff suggestions for change (one of the suggestions made by a staff member was for more flexible and longer working hours, to suit consumers); set quantitative goals for consumer-oriented performance standards (e.g. 90 per cent of applications will receive their first payment within 30 days) and built these into management contracts within the department; and developed a quality measure for errors (in calculating benefit, issuing cheques etc.) whereby an ever-decreasing score is set for the ten area units. With regard to that last point, it is significant to note that the error scores are calculated regularly by a special independent checking team that examines case files, but the scores are not seen by the director; they are seen only by local managers who are expected (and trusted) to take steps to improve their error score.

The Association of Municipal Authorities in the Netherlands did a series of studies of social services departments in the country's cities and towns, the second in the series happening to come about two-thirds of the way through the VONK project. The results showed that Groningen went from near the bottom of the list on various criteria, to near the top.

But Groningen found that quality costs. In addition to

the direct costs of the project (training, management consultancy etc), higher salaries were negotiated for staff to match higher reponsibilities. At a time when 5 million guilders was cut from the municipal budget, VONK cost the city 2 million guilders for the first 18 months of operation.

One further point to note: an attempt at direct participation by consumers in the VONK project failed. In the early stages, a 10-person consumer panel was set up to visit various municipal departments "in disguise" as ordinary consumers, to monitor the VONK project, see how staff deal with the public etc. When staff discovered this was happening, there was a furore, and the consumer panel ceased to function.

UK Computerised Welfare Benefits Project

In the early 1980's, the UK Department of Health and Social Security tested a project that addressed the chronic problem of consumers' lack of information about services and cash benefits available to them, a problem which results in low take-up of those services and benefits.

The Department installed nine experimental microcomputers in various places throughout the UK - community centres, government offices, and in one case a supermarket. These micro's were specially programmed to enable ordinary people to find out by themselves, without training on computers or help from staff, exactly what they were entitled to and how to claim it. Of course staff at the agencies could also use it if they wanted, either to work out benefits for their clients or to suggest to their clients that they use it. The computers were simply placed there, in accessible public areas, to see what would happen.

When not in use, a permanent message flashed on the screen, inviting people, if they had 25 minutes to spare, to find out if they were entitled to claim anything just by sitting down and pressing the button marked "start".

This was putting the power of information technology literally at the fingertips of the consumer, with no intermediary. Evaluation (49) showed that, contrary to many predictions, all kinds of people were happy to try the computer: young and old, male and female. Users were, in the vast majority of cases, people in difficult financial circumstances, usually with no job and no higher education.

And they enjoyed getting information direct from the computer, as the following sample of consumer comments shows:

"Super, easy as pie. First time we used one. No problems at all"

"I think it's great. I just think it's good to find out your rights. You can do it yourself. It gives you the feeling you're doing something"

"Very good. If I can use it, anybody can. I 'phoned up twice (to the government agency) and all I got was a load of abuse..." (49)

Although most computer users had already tried to find out their entitlement in some other way (asking a staff member, reading a leaflet etc.) over half (60 per cent) discovered, from the computer, they were entitled to something they were not receiving. Of those, half had actually followed through with a claim one month later, which in nearly all cases was granted.

So, from the consumer point of view, the computers were a success. The computers gave them information they had not known before. But staff in the public sector agencies in which the computers were placed had a different perspective, and a rather less enthusiastic response to the computers.

In the case of social security offices, a national union agreement laid out the terms under which staff would agree to the computers being placed in the office. Those terms were that counter staff were to have nothing whatsoever to do with the computer. At one of the offices, there was even a sign placed next to the computer telling users not to disturb the counter clerk.

At social service departments, the reaction of social workers was more mixed, but still generally negative. Two sets of reactions in particular stood out. One was that social workers felt consumers had no need of the computer because they - the social workers - could tell their clients all they needed to know. But the research showed that despite their contact with social workers, consumers were uninformed about their entitlements until they used the computer.

The second major theme was that computers were unsuitable for consumers of social work services, either because consumers with social problems are too stressed to use a computer or because they were not intelligent enough to use a computer. Both of these objections were belied by the results.

Consumer-operated benefit computers have since been discontinued by the government.

Spain Ministry for Public Administration

In 1987, the Service Operations Inspection initiative (SOI) was begun in Spain's central administration. SOI is intended to promote flexible, more effective and more accessible services and to improve administration/consumer relations. Those responsible for this initiative acknowledge the inspiration provided by the commercial sector, in seeking a more dynamic model for the public services.

SOI is basically an evaluation and monitoring system that both enables and encourages public sector managers to collect and use consumer data to improve their services: a performance assessment system.

The Ministry has selected five departments in which to introduce SOI including social security, education and health; it will be expanded to other agencies at a later date. In any department, or sub-section of a department, in which it is introduced, SOI involves four stages:

- preliminary data collection and staff interviews to identify major service problems;

- detailed study and field research with consumers;

- analysis of data, arriving at conclusions and drawing up recommendations for change in organisational structure and coordination of procedures (with special emphasis on how to reduce waiting times for service by members of the public, already identified as a general problem); and

- an implementation plan, including personal staff responsibilities and specific time framework for implementation.

SOI is an initiative of a central agency - the Ministry for Public Administration - but all four stages are completed in close collaboration with the individual service departments involved so that each manager "owns" the ideas.

The first service where SOI was introduced was in welfare benefits for the elderly and disabled. As a result of the analysis, surveys and group meetings held with both staff and consumers, a plan was developed to simplify procedures, standardise documents across the different directorates of the service, make better use of data provided by applicants rather than asking for the same information over and over again, reduce the number of documents required from benefit claimants, and develop a Procedures Manual to promote greater administrative professionalisation among staff. Maximum time targets were also set for paying out benefits to consumers.

In the health service, out-patients departments (OPDS) were given the SOI treatment. In all, 14 OPDs in 11 provinces were looked at, and over 2,000 patients interviewed. What emerged was a plan to coordinate services to patients by reorganising all medical specialities under one organisational unit; to produce an Appointments Manual, training staff on how to operate an appointments-based service; to coordinate various medical test appointments, for the convenience of the patient; to provide training courses in human resources for those staff in direct contact with consumers; and to correct the shortage of material resources, particularly in new technology.

At the time of writing, all SOI plans were just approaching the implementation stage (stage 4).

Orebo Home Help and Kent Community Care

In the city of Orebo, Sweden, and in the county of Kent, England, similar initiatives in autonomy for front line workers have been tried recently. In both authorities, employee participation was regarded as an essential part of the strategy to improve the consumer effectiveness of the public sector.

In Orebo, teams of five to eight home helps organised and managed home care services for clients. A senior staff person was available to act as a resource, if needed. The home helps had complete responsibility not only for providing home care services, but for every other function as well: record keeping, liaising with other authorities, answering the 'phone, and allocating financial and manpower resources.

Evaluation showed that, when compared to a control (a traditional hierarchical home care team), the Orebo teams were found to perform 67 per cent of all advisory, planning and liaison activities, compared to only ten per cent for the control team. The Orebo teams were characterised by more exchanges of knowledge within the team than controls, more freedom to reorganise services according to need, and more feedback from consumers. The views of consumers were unfortunately not sought in the evaluation, but in the Orebo worker participation teams one-half of the workers claimed to be familiar with the family situation of clients, compared to only one-quarter of the traditional teams. In the worker participation teams, furthermore, there was greater willingness to see consumers outside normal working hours; less distaste for visiting difficult elderly clients; and a greater tendency to regard clients as equals. Although jobs were viewed as more demanding, they were also viewed as more satisfying.

Similarly, in Kent, frontline workers—this time social workers—were given greater autonomy in delivering community care to the elderly in order to achieve a more consumer-responsive service. Control over a budget was found to give the social workers a real incentive to undertake more careful assessments of need, and to devise original solutions to problems. Staff felt freer, too, to involve the consumers themselves in decisions, because of this new sense of control over resources.

Considerable differences were found amongst consumers receiving the services of the autonomous workers in Kent and a matched control group getting standard social work services. Consumers in the special scheme scored higher on subjective measures of well-being, and expressed a stronger desire to remain in their own homes than to be taken into residential care. Perhaps most important, in the third year of the Kent scheme, one-third of the elderly were still in their own homes, compared to only ten per cent of the "standard" consumers. Devolved authority, combined with smaller case loads, high skills, and control of a decentralised budget, not only encouraged ingenuity in developing a successful package of coordinated services to the consumer, but cost analysis, in Kent, showed it was actually less expensive for the authority.

Harlow Complaints Procedure

The town of Harlow, in England, has developed and implemented a formal consumer complaints handling procedure for all its services, which include housing, community services, leisure, roads and others.

The complaints procedure was instituted in 1988, and was developed with two purposes in mind:

- to make public services more open and accessible to consumers

- to fulfil a quality control function - receiving and monitoring complaints was seen as an important element in developing high quality services.

The complaints procedure was formulated in consultation with staff, particularly frontline staff. In all, about 20 briefing sessions were held with staff and in the end a detailed note on the procedures to be followed on receipt of a complaint was circulated to staff.

To initiate a complaint, a consumer must fill in a brief and very simple complaint form that is attached to a leaflet explaining the authority's complaint procedure. The leaflet is entitled "Hitting your head against a brick wall?" and 10,000 copies were distributed to libraries, community centres, health centres, council offices etc. The leaflet was also publicised in the local newspaper which goes to every household in Harlow.

Once a complaint form is received, a multi-stage

process is invoked, which specifies time limits placed on officers to respond, how the complaint should be investigated, recording procedures for monitoring complaints, and appeals procedures. These start from the Head of Department, through the General Manager and finally the Appeals Committee, which consumers must be informed of if they are unsatisfied with the outcome at any stage.

In practice, the authority has found that most complaints are settled at an early stage, and in the first year of operation only 20 have gone beyond the Head of Department.

All complaints are entered into a case record sheet, summarising the nature of the complaint and what happened to it. Statistics are regularly monitored and fed into statutory departmental policy review processes, instituting procedures that will prevent complaints from arising in the first place. In at least two instances so far, complaints have resulted in altering procedures for inter-authority coordination.

Nord-Pas de Calais Region

There are a number of initiatives taking place at regional level and at more local levels in this area in northern France, including developments in Lille and other neighbouring towns. They serve to illustrate activity in France, which tends to concentrate on improving information to consumers of public services.

In recent years, France has passed a number of laws to guarantee consumer rights to information in the public sector, e.g.:

- access to their file documents
- the right of reply to every written communication from consumers
- requiring the name of the responsible official to appear on all written correspondence.

These legal developments have shaped - or perhaps been shaped by - interest in improving reception and information arrangements at regional, town hall, department and prefecture level.

An examination of developments in the Nord-Pas de Calais region shows that there have been some very welcome developments locally. For example, "hostesses" were introduced with the specific purpose of improving reception and information for the consumer at many public offices, and training was given on relations with the public. The training, however, was limited only to the receptionists; no other level of staff in contact with the public is given training in delivering services.

At the prefecture, two staff members have been employed to provide translation services for communicating with ethnic minorities. The department has a representative of the "Mediateur" service one half day per week, to handle complaints, which are mostly about benefit payments. The town of Lille also has a mediator service dealing mainly with housing problems.

Lille's mediation service is highly accessible to the public - just inside the main town hall entrance. Or at least the reception desk is accessible - the service itself used to be at the entrance too, but had to be moved out of sight, further into the building, because of the occasional dust-up caused by consumers getting disappointing advice.

The municipal administration of Lille was decentralised with 10 mini-town halls completed in 1987, and the emphasis in decentralisation has been on improving the availability of information to the neighbourhood. Each mini-town hall can provide information not only on municipal services but also on services provided by other levels of government, particularly the prefecture. The heads of each mini-town hall, and the staff, are recruited particularly for their abilities to communicate and for their familiarity with local services and conditions. An opinion poll conducted recently showed that relations between the municipal administration and the public have improved since decentralisation, and the number of people who use the various services has risen.

Since 1982, Lille has had a CIRA office which in 1986 answered about 90,000 calls for information on virtually every area of public service. CIRA is staffed by 15 officials temporarily seconded from the different ministries, so that it can give expert advice in every field.

CIRA advises only by telephone. The various administrative levels also make information available locally on Minitel - over 150,000 Minitels have been provided in the region - though not all information sources feed into Minitel (e.g. the prefecture).

The area also has AVS, "A votre service" (at your service), a consumer help and information programme first piloted in France in 1982. It was set up in four parts of the country, including the Nord-Pas de Calais region, where several towns have an AVS; the AVS in Bethune is a simple booth staffed by three people, "locals" familiar with the area. Some AVS's have a local liaison committee of consumers and professionals that acts as a steering group. AVS cuts across and coordinates information about all public services. It responds to requests for information by 'phone, mail, and in person, and is supported by a database on Minitel.

But it does more than give information; it also assumes a more activist, interventionist role on behalf of consumers, providing practical help in filling out forms, acting as an advocate in dealing with other officials and writing letters on the client's behalf. The AVS in Bethune averages ten requests for help a day, and sometimes receives as many as 30 a day.

After announcing in 1983 that AVS would be extended to every region, plans for expansion were abruptly dropped in 1986 and AVS ceased to be an "Official" project. It continues only if the local prefect is personally interested.

A German Experimental Approach to Consumer Participation

At the University of Wuppertal, a method of involving consumers in public sector decision-making, developed and tested by Peter Dienel, has been implemented as far afield as New Jersey, USA (in 1988).

There have been a number of criticisms directed at usual forms of consumer participation: consumers lack specialised or technical knowledge about service delivery; it is difficult to stimulate interest in participation; those who participate may not be representative of consumers as a whole; certain groups are chronically underrepresented in consumer consultative groups.

To answer such criticisms, Dienel has developed a system based on what he terms the "planning cell". Planning cells are groups of citizens chosen at random from population registers, and granted paid leave from their normal obligations for two to five days in order to work out solutions to problems. Subject experts are available throughout for questions, discussion, information.

A single problem, usually related to environmental or public planning issues, may be looked at by many planning cells. For example, one project on energy supply had 24 cells throughout Germany. Each cell may contain about five people.

At the end of the specified period, reports are prepared presenting the consumer view of the solution to the problem. A consolidated report, presenting the overview of all the cells, is prepared by a (neutral) member of the university research team.

The kinds of problems on which this approach has been tested have included waste disposal sites, rebuilding a historic town area, highway routing, planning recreation areas, use of information technology. It is a form of intensive market research but one in which ordinary consumer preferences regarding highly complex issues can be tapped, and the underlying reasons for attitudes can be ascertained.

The planning cell approach has generated ideas and alternatives "rather different from those which emerge from official planning" (60). It is seen, by its originators, not as a substitute for other methods of consumer participation but rather as a supplement, to add its own unique dimension.

BIBLIOGRAPHY

(1) Allen, I. (ed), 'Hearing the voice of the consumer' Policy Studies Institute 1988

(2) Andreani, J-L., and Vernholes, A., 'Un entretien avec M. Michel Rocard', *Le Monde*, 24 February 1989

(3) Association pour l'Amelioration des Rapports entre l'Administration et le Public, 'Publics et services publics - un nouveau dialogue', colloque de 20 Mai 1987, ARAP, Paris, 1987

(4) Association pour l'Amelioration des Rapports entre l'Administration et le Public, *Actualités*, No. 25 May 1988

(5) Association pour l'Amelioration des Rapports entre l'Administration et le Public, *Actualites*, No. 26, September 1988

(6) Baddeley, S., and Dawes, N., 'Service to the customer - the secrets of front line/back line training', paper presented at a RIPA seminar 'Clients, managers and public services', 27 November 1985

(7) Baddeley, S., and Dawes, N., 'Information technology support for devolution - vision and reality in Walsall Housing Department', *Local Government Studies*, July/August 1987, pp 1-16

(8) Baldersheim, H., and Rose, L., 'Lessons and paradoxes from ten years of assessing citizen satisfaction with public services in Norway - and presentation of a new research initiative', paper presented at OECD/IULA Conference, 'Urban services and consumer needs', Amsterdam, 22-25 April 1988

(9) Berwick, S., " 'Unacceptable' service by DHSS", *Independent*, 24 June 1988

(10) Becher, U., and Gaspary H., 'Kooperationsmodell Derendorf', projekt No. 10, Zweiter Jahresbericht zur Vorlage bei der EG-Kommission, December 1987

(11) Beishon, J., 'Empowering consumers', *New Socialist*, June/July 1989, pp 16-17

(12) Benjamin, A., 'Communicating with customers', *Local Government Chronicle Supplement*, 22 April p 3

(13) Berdowski, Z., 'Municipal department of statistics and research" paper presented at OECD/IULA Conference, Urban services and consumer needs', Amsterdam, 22-25 April, 1988

(14) 'Biggest of all Government advertising', *Economist*, 30 April 1988, p 36

(15) Bingley, W., 'Advocacy and consumers: "The Advocacy Alliance" ', in Clode, D., Parker, C., and Etherington, S., (eds), 'Towards the sensitive bureaucracy - consumers, welfare and the new pluralism', Gower, 1987

(16) Birkinshaw, P., 'Departments of state, citizens and the internal resolution of grievances', *Civil Justice Quarterly*, Vol 4, January 1985, pp 15-48

(17) BMRB, internal report, DHSS Working Papers, 17 February 1986

(18) Brindle, D., 'Social security staff offered "divisive" bonus scheme', *Guardian*, 21 June 1989

(19) Cabinet Office, 'Customer service - a philosophy not a department', report of a Conference held at Wolfson College, Oxford, 19 June 1987

(20) Cabinet Office, 'Service to the Public', Occasional Paper, HMSO, December 1988

(21) Cadbury, D., 'Establishing a mental handicap register', *Physiotherapy*, Vol 71, No 4, April 1985

(22) Carr-Hill, R., Humphreys, K., and McIver, S., 'A customised view of public satisfaction', *Health Services Journal*, 28 May 1987, pp 614-615

(23) Challis, D., 'Case management and consumer choice: "The Kent community care scheme" ', in Clode, D., Parker, C., and Etherington S., (eds), 'Towards the sensitive bureaucracy - consumers, welfare and the new pluralism', Gower, 1987

(24) City & Hackney Community Health Council, 'Experiments in health advocacy - multi-ethnic health project', July 1988

(25) Clarke, M., 'The approach of the Local Government Training Board in England and Wales', paper presented at OECD/IULA Conference, 'Urban services and consumer needs', Amsterdam, 22-25 April, 1988

(26) Clarke, M., and Stewart, J., 'The service programme: report on a visit to Sweden', Local Government and Public Service: Working Paper 2, Local Government Training Board, 1985

(27) Clarke, M., and Stewart, J., 'The public service orientation - developing the approach', Working Paper 3, Local Government Training Board, April 1986

(28) Clarke, M., and Stewart, J., 'The public service orientation and the citizen', *Local Government Policy Making*, Vol 14 No. I June 1987, pp 34-40

(29) Clifton, N., 'Public health - personal service: it ain't what you do it's the way that you do it' in Epstein, J., et al, 'Providing public services that serve the public - report on an Anglo-German conference', Anglo-German Foundation for the Study of Industrial Society, 1989

(30) Clode, D., Parker, C., and Etherington, S., (eds), 'Towards the sensitive bureaucracy - consumers, welfare and the new pluralism', Gower, 1987

(31) Community Projects Foundation, 'Public involvement in local government - a survey in England and Wales', 1985

(32) Consumers' Association, 'Primary health care - an agenda for discussion', May 1987

(33) Cook, T., 'Participation', in Clode, D., Parker, C., and Etherington, S.,(eds), 'Towards the sensitive bureaucracy - consumer, Welfare and the new pluralism', Gower, 1987

(34) Coupe, M., 'Reflections on the Dutch experience', *Health Services Management* No. 3 Vol 18, June 1988, pp 24-27

(35) Davies, H., Discussion paper presented at OECD/IULA Conference, 'Urban services and consumer needs', Amsterdam 22-25, April 1988

(36) Davies, H., Comments during workshop discussion, OECD/IULA Conference, 'Urban services and consumer needs', Amsterdam 22-25 April 1988

(37) de Graff, H., 'Computers in the Dutch Social Services', paper presented at HUSITA Conference, *Computer Applications in Social Work,* Vol 3 No. 4 Autumn 1987, pp 15-19

(38) Dean, M., 'Consumer interests of the Tories', *Guardian,* 12 August 1988, p 19

(39) Deiters, R., 'The work of the Federal Employment Institute', in Epstein, J., et al, 'Providing public services that serve the public report on an Anglo-German conference', Anglo-German Foundation for the Study of Industrial Society, 1989

(40) Department of Health and Social Security, 'Service to the public: a handbook of good practice', HMSO, 1983

(41) Department of Social Security, 'Service to the public: a handbook of good practice', 2nd edition, DSS, 1988

(42) Direction Departmentale des Affaires Sanitaires et Sociales, 'Chartre de la qualité', Nantes, 27 June 1988

(43) Drucker, P., 'The practice of management', Heinemann, London, 1955

(44) Ellis, R., 'Quality assurance: the professional's role', *Public Money and Management,* Vol 8 Nos. 1 and 2 spring/summer 1988, pp 7-40

(45) Employment and Immigration Canada, 'Memorandum of understanding on Ministerial authority and accountability', 1988

(46) Epstein, J., 'Consumer Research', *Journal of Consumer Studies and Home Economics,* 3, 1979, pp 269-276

(47) Epstein, J., 'Consumer Research, Part II - Discussion of

five more consumer topics and suggestions for future research', *Journal of Consumer Studies and Home Economics,* 4, 1980, pp 51-60
(48) Epstein, J., 'Consumer assessment of an experiment in supplementary benefit claims', Research Institute for Consumer Affairs, 1982
(49) Epstein, J., 'New technology - new entitlement?: An experiment in public-access computers to assess entitlement to benefit', Research Institute for Consumer Affairs, April 1984
(50) Epstein, J., 'Review of European Foundation research on new technology: computers and the consumer', Research Institute for Consumer Affairs, August 1986
(51) Epstein, J., 'Providing information about urban services' booklet No. 3, European Foundation for the Improvement of Living and Working Conditions, 1987
(52) Epstein, J., 'Information systems and the consumer', in Glastonbury, B., La Mendola, W., and Toole, S., (eds), 'Information technology and the human services', John Wiley & Sons, 1988
(53) Epstein, J., 'Consumer information about urban services', paper presented at OECD/IULA Conference, 'Urban services and consumer needs', Amsterdam, 22-25 April, 1988
(54) Epstein, J., et al, 'Providing public services that serve the public-report on an Anglo-German conference', Anglo-German Foundation for the Study of Industrial Society, 1989
(55) *Exchange,* Programme of the European Communities to Combat Poverty, No. 9, November 1988
(56) Fabian Society, Policy review, discussion paper No 1, May 1988
(57) Flynn, N., 'A consumer-oriented culture', *Public Money and Management,* Vol 8, Nos 1 & 2 spring/ summer 1988, pp 27-31
(58) Federation Generale Autonome des Fonctionnaires and Syndicat National Unifie des Impots, 'Plaidoyer pour un service public - Des fonctionnaires s'expriment', FGAF/SNUI, 1987
(59) Foers, J., 'Forms design: an international perspective - a comparative study of government administrative forms', Inland Revenue, February 1987
(60) Garbe, D., 'Planning cell and citizen report: a report on German experiences with new participation instruments', *European Journal of Political Research,* 14, 1986 pp 221-236
(61) Gaspary, H., letter, 30 March 1989

(62) Glastonbury, B., La Mendola, W., and Toole, S., (eds), 'Information technology and human services', John Wiley & Sons, 1988

(63) Goodwin, N., 'Implementing customer awareness at unit level', *Hospital and Health Services Review*. vol 83 No. 6, November 1987, pp 248-251

(64) Griffin, A., 'Customer care must not be neglected', *Local Government Chronicle*, 22 April 1988, p 19

(65) Griffin, A., 'Keeping service delivery in sight', *Local Government Chronicle*, 26 August, 1988, p 15

(66) Griffiths, R., 'Does the public service serve? - the consumer dimension', Royal Institute of Public Administration Redcliffe-Maud Memorial Lecture, 29 June 1987

(67) Griffiths, R., 'Does the public service serve? The consumer dimension', *Public Administration*, Vol 66, No 2, summer 1988, pp 195-204

(68) Groningen Municipal Government, 'About bananas, an investment, and council employees doing their best' (undated)

(69) Grunow, D., 'Methods and problems of research into the relationship between urban services and consumers', paper presented at OECD/IULA conference, 'Urban services and consumer needs', Amsterdam, 22-25 April, 1988

(70) Grunow, D., 'Public services: the current state of development in West Germany', in Epstein, J., et al, 'Providing public services that serve the public - report on an Anglo-German conference', Anglo-German Foundation for the study of industrial society, 1989

(71) Gustafsson, L., 'Improving political control of administration: aspects of the Swedish public sector renewal programme', unpublished paper

(72) Gustafsson, L., 'Renewal of the public sector in Sweden', *Public Administration*, Vol 65, No 2, Summer 1987

(73) Hadley, R., and Hugman R., 'Organisation know thyself', *Community Care*, issue 747, 26 January 1989, pp 20-21

(74) Hambleton, R., and Hoggett, P., (eds), 'The politics of decentralisation: theory and practice of a radical local government initiative', Working paper No 46, University of Bristol School for Advanced Urban Studies, 1984

(75) Hambleton, R., 'Consumerism, decentralization and local democracy', *Public Administration*, Vol 66, No. 2, Summer 1988 pp 125-147

(76) Hambleton, R., 'Reflections on current trends in Britain and America', Paper presented at Royal Institute of

Public Administration and Community Projects Foundation conference 'Managing the public services', London, 23 June 1989

(77) Handy, C., 'How to lead the smart organisation', *Sunday Times,* 23 April 1989

(78) Hatry, H., 'Gearing the provision of urban services to consumer needs', The Urban Institute, Washington, DC, USA, December 1987

(79) Heery, E., 'A common labour movement? Left Labour councils and the trade unions', in Hoggett, P., and Hambleton, R., (eds) 'Decentralisation and democracy - localising public services', Occasional paper 28, School for Advanced Urban Studies, University of Bristol, 1987

(80) Hill, M., 'Better service in public services', paper presented at Family Service Unit/Royal Institute of Public Administration conference, 30 March 1984

(81) Hodson, G., and Ray, A., 'Contribution by Wakefield Metropolitan District Council', paper presented at the OECD/IULA Conference, 'Urban services and consumer needs', Amsterdam, 22-25 April 1988

(82) Hoggett, P., and Hambleton, R., (eds), 'Decentralisation and democracy - localising public services', Occasional paper 28, School of Advanced Urban Studies, University of Bristol, 1987, pp 194-214

(83) Hoyland, P., 'Solihull gets hot line to council chief', *Guardian,* 14 September, 1987, pp3

(84) Institut Francais des Sciences Administratives, 'La transformation des relations entre l'administration et les usagers', Paris, 1988

(85) Irish Government, 'Serving the country better: a White Paper on the public service', Stationery Office, Dublin 1985

(86) Islington Council, 'Going local - decentralisaton in practice', Islington Council, December 1986

(87) Islington Council, 'Report to the decentralisation working group', 30 May 1989

(88) James, A., 'Performance and the planning process', *Social Services Insight,* 6 March, 1987, pp 12-14

(89) Jones, A., 'Collaboration with consumers: learning how to listen', in Allen, I., (ed) 'Hearing the voice of the consumer', Policy Studies Institute, 1988, pp 53-61

(90) Kerruish, A., Wickings, I., and Tarrant, P., 'Information from patients as a management tool - empowering managers to improve the quality of care', *Hospital and Health Services Review* Vol 84, No. 2, April 1988, pp 64-67

(91) King, D., 'Health', in Clode, D., Parker, C., and

Etherington, S., (eds), 'Towards the sensitive bureaucracy - consumers, welfare and the new pluralism', Gower, 1987

(92) Kings Fund, 'Living well into old age - applying principles of good practice to services for people with dementia', Project paper 63, Kings Fund, 1986

(93) Kirkpatrick, J., 'Consumer strategy in the public sector: are you being served', *Public Money and Management*, Vol 8 Nos. I & 2, spring/ summer 1988, pp 41-43

(94) Klein, R., 'The politics of participation', in Maxwell, R., and Weaver, N., (eds), 'Public participation in health: towards a clearer view', Kings Fund, 1984, pp 17-32

(95) Koetzsche, H., 'Improving the Hamburg police service' in Epstein, J., et al, 'Providing public services that serve the public - report on an Anglo-German conference', Anglo-German Foundation for the Study of Industrial Society, 1989

(96) Kroppenstedt, F., 'Der gesetzliche Hintergrund in der Bundesrepublik Deutschland', in Epstein, J., et al, 'Providing public services that serve the public - report on an Anglo-German conference', Anglo-German Foundation for the Study of Industrial Society, 1989

(97) Leabeter, D., 'Developing consumer responsiveness', paper presented at the OCED/IULA Conference, 'Urban services and consumer needs', Amsterdam, 22-25 April 1988

(98) Lemmens, C., Pauka, T., '''t Kon Minder tekenen van verandering in de ambtelijke cultuur van de gemeente Groningen'', Gemeente Groningen, 1988

(99) Lewis, N., Seneviratne, S., and Cracknell, S., 'Complaints procedures in local government', Centre for Criminological and Socio-Legal Studies, University of Sheffield, 1987

(100) Local Government Training Board, 'Has marketing a role in local government? - a discussion paper', LGTB, 1985

(101) Local Government Training Board, 'Getting closer to the public', LGTB, 1987

(102) Local Government Training Board, 'Learning from the public', LGTB, 1988

(103) Mainwaring, R., 'The Walsall experience - a study of the decentralisation of Walsall's housing service', HMSO, 1988

(104) Martin, E., 'Consumer evaluation of human services', *Social Policy & Administration*, Vol 20 No 3, Autumn 1986, pp 185-199

(105) May, A., 'Measure for Measure', *Health Services Journal*, 8 September 1988, pp 1028-1029

(106) May, A., 'Encoding the principles of good practice', *Health Services Journal*, 10 November 1988, pp322

(107) Ministere de la Fonction Publique et du Plan, 'Administration 88: rencontres nationales de l'innovation et de la qualite', *Le Zenith*, Paris, 13 January 1988

(108) Ministerio Para las Administraciones Publicas, 'Inspecciones Operativas de Servicios', Madrid, November 1988

(109) Murray, P., Seminar at the Royal Institute of Public Administration, London, 21 January, 1987

(110) National Consumer Council, 'Measuring up - consumer assessment of local authority services: a guideline study', NCC, 1986

(111) National Consumer Council, 'Assessing consumers' experiences of the National Health Service: outline of work to be conducted by the National Consumer Council with reference to services for elderly people suffering from dementia', August 1987

(112) National Consumer Council and National Institute for Social Work, 'Open to complaints: guidelines for social services complaints procedures', NCC, 1988

(113) Observer Education Staff, 'Good school guide angers teachers' *Observer,* 5 June, 1988, p 8

(114) Organisation for Economic Cooperation and Development, 'Administration as service; the public as client', OECD, Paris, 1987

(115) Organisation for Economic Cooperation and Development, 'A survey of initiatives for improving relationships between the citizen and the administration', *Public Management Studies* No.1, OECD, Paris 1987

(116) Organisation for Economic Cooperation and Development, 'Administrative responsiveness and employment services', *Public Management Studies* No.3, OECD, Paris 1988

(117) Organisation for Economic Cooperation and Development, 'Recent trends in performance, appraisal and performance-related pay schemes in the public service', *Public Management Studies* No. 4, OECD, Paris, 1988

(118) Organisation for Economic Cooperation and Development/International Union of Local Authorities, 'Urban services and consumer needs', workshop papers, Amsterdam, 22-25 April 1988

(119) Pauka, T., and Zunderforp, R., 'De banaan wordt bespreekbaar: cultuurverandering in ambtelijk en politiek Groningen', Nijgh & Van Ditmar, 1988

(120) Peschek, D., 'Image', *Local Government Chronicle*, 9 October 1987, p 22

(121) Peters, T., and Waterman, R., 'In search of excellence: lessons from America's best run companies', Harper & Row, New York, 1982

(122) Pollitt, C., 'Bringing consumers into performance measurement: concepts, consequences and constraints', *Policy and Politics*, No. 2 Vol 16, April 1988, pp 77-87

(123) Pollitt, C., (ed), 'Consumerism and beyond' (Theme Issue), *Public Administration*, Vol 66, No 2, summer 1988

(124) Potter, J., 'Consumerism and the public sector: how well does the coat fit?', *Public Administration*, Vol 66, No 2, summer 1988 pp149-164

(125) Pratt, K., 'Customer services and the One Stop experience', paper presented at OECD/IULA Conference, 'Urban services and consumer needs', Amsterdam, 22-25 April 1988

(126) Rae Price, J., 'Decentralisation - and though it in the centre sit...', *Social Services Insight*, 15 May, 1987, pp 12-14

(127) Richardson, A., 'Participation' concepts in social policy 1, Routledge & Kegan Paul, 1983

(128) Richardson, A., and Bray, C., 'Promoting health through participation: experience of groups for patient participation in general practice', research report no. 659, Policy Studies Institute, 1987

(129) Royal Institute of Public Administration, 'Focus on health care', RIPA, 1988

(130) Royal Institute of Public Administration and Community Projects Foundation, 'Managing the public services: involving the disadvantaged consumer', one day conference, London, 23 June 1989

(131) Sang, B., and O'Brien, J., 'Advocacy - the UK and American experiences', Project Paper 51, Kings Fund, London 1987

(132) Secretariado para a Modernizacao Administrative, publicity flyer for seminar, Lisbon, 10-11 March 1988

(133) Seneviratne, M., and Cracknell, S., 'Consumer complaints in public sector services', *Public Administration*, Vol 66, No 2, summer 1988, pp 181-193

(134) Scrivens, E., 'Improving customer awareness: evaluating an approach', *Public Money and Management*, Vol 8 Nos 1 & 2 spring/summer 1988, pp 33-35

(135) Silvestre, M., 'Conflict and collaboration strategies for

the promotion of innovation', Report presented at the Conference of the European Programme to Combat Poverty, 'Elderly Persons' Transnational Team Meeting, Rome, 24-25 May 1987

(136) Smith, J., 'Achieving change in the personal social services', in Epstein, J., et al 'Providing services that serve the public', Report on an Anglo-German Conference, Anglo German Foundation for the Study of Industrial Society, 1989

(137) Smith, J., 'Social Services', in Clode, D., Parker, C., and Etherington, S., (eds) 'Towards the Sensitive Bureaucracy: consumers, welfare and the new pluralism', Gower, 1987

(138) Smith, J., 'Service users - clients, users, consumers and members', *Local Government Policy Making,* March 1985, pp 77-82

(139) Smith, M., 'The consumer case for socialism', Fabian Tract 513, Fabian Society, July 1986

(140) Social Services Research Group, 'Performance measurement in personal social services', *Research Policy and Planning,* Vol 6, No 2, 1988, pp 1-47

(141) Spindler, L., 'Discussion paper: urban services and consumer needs', in OECD/IULA Conference, 'Urban services and consumer needs', Amsterdam, 22-25 April 1988

(142) Stewart, J., and Clarke, M., 'The public service orientation: issues and dilemmas', *Public Administration,* Vol 65, No. 2, Summer 1987, pp 161-177

(143) Stoker, G., Oppenheim, F., and Davies, M., 'The challenge of change in local government: a survey of organisational and management innovation in the 1980s', Institute of Local Government Studies, University of Birmingham, May 1988

(144) Thom, B., 'New approaches in welfare administration', Paper presented at the Seminar 'Getting back to people', Zwolle, The Netherlands, 26 Sept - 2 Oct 1982, The European Centre, Vienna, 1983

(145) Timmins, N., 'Family doctors reject "easier complaints" ', *Independent,* 24 October 1986, p 3

(146) Tower Hamlets, press release, 14 October 1986

(147) Vernholes, A., 'Le plan de renovation du service public prevoit une formation renforcee des responsables', *Le Mond,* 23 February, 1989

(148) von Otter, C., 'Responsiveness in public service organizations, the case for "public competition" and "participative management"', paper presented to OECD/

IULA Conference, 'Urban services and consumer needs', Amsterdam 22-25 April 1988

(149) Welsh Consumer Council, 'Consulting claimants: a study of consumer participation in the social security service', Welsh Consumer Council, July 1987

(150) Westminster, City of, 'City of Westminster One Stop - innovation in services provision' (undated)

(151) Whitting, G., Henningsen, B., and Tricart, J., 'Social institutions and social protection', European Poverty Programme, Key issue paper, University of Bath, February 1989

(152) Williamson, C., 'Reviewing the quality of care in the National Health Service', National Association of Health Authorities, 1987

(153) Williamson, V., 'Patients first - reality or rhetoric?', *Social Policy & Administration,* Vol 22, No 3, December 1988, pp 245-258

(154) Willmott, P., (ed), 'Local government decentralisation and community', Policy Studies Institute, 1987

(155) Willoughby, C., 'Administration without bureaucratisation', Introductory talk at IIAS conference in Budapest, September 1988

(156) Winkler, F., 'Consumerism in health care: beyond the supermarket model', *Policy and Politics,* pp 1-8, Vol 15 No. 1, 1987

(157) Winkler, F., 'Post the Review - community/consumer representation in the NHS', Greater London Association of Community Health Councils, February 1989

(158) Woods, P., 'Understanding consumer participation', paper presented at OECD/IULA Conference, 'Urban services and consumer needs', Amsterdam 22-25 April 1988

Other Relevant Foundation Publications

Building for People in Hospitals: Workers and Consumers (1990)

The organisation and functions of health service buildings affect the working conditions of staff and the quality of care for patients. The papers in this report examine how the daily life of hospital workers and consumers are shaped by the built environment and how these health institutions can become more conducive to health. The papers draw upon experience of new building and renovation in Europe to illustrate the contribution of user participation in the design. They will interest policy-makers and health service administrators, as well as planners and architects, who aim to design and rehabilitate the hospitals in the interest of both healthier work and improved service. (Published in English only).

SY-58-90-376-EN-C   ECU 20.00

Social Change and Local Action (1990)

Local community action is increasingly being recognised as a strategy for raising the quality of life. At the neighbourhood level, people are being drawn into partnerships with the public, private and voluntary sector. A vast range of groups and organisations with diverse structures and methods are taking action to meet environmental, social and economic needs. However, to date, there has been little basic research which identifies the policies and processes which make effective local action possible. This report asks what are the relative strenghts and weaknesses of local action, what resources and support systems are required, who participates and who benefits? It aims to clarify the ideas and the mechanisms for increasing local involvement in bringing about improvements in the quality of life. (Published in EN,FR, NL,ES,PT).

SY-57-89-338-EN-C   ECU 7.50

Providing Information About Urban Services (1990)

Many people in high risk population groups do not know about services available to help them. This booklet is intended to encourage agencies to devote more resources to the development of effective ways of getting information to those who need it. (Published in all Community languages).

SY-48-87-371-EN-C   ECU 5.90

Living Conditions in Urban Europe (1988)

An overview of current European policy relevant to urban living conditions, this booklet summarizes the impact of social and economic changes on the structure of cities and the quality of life in urban Europe. Trends in demography, family life, labour markets, housing provision and community involvement are examined and particular attention is paid to the processes of marginalization which are creating and reinforcing social inequalities within cities. (published in all Community languages).

SY-48-87-315-EN-C   ECU 4.70

Growing Up and Leaving Home (1989)

For a significant minority of young people it is not easy to manage the transition from dependent to independent living and some form of homelessness is experienced. Young people without extensive family resources to draw upon are particularily vulnerable. Many who want to leave home, often in search of work, cannot do so because of a lack of suitable and affordable housing. This information booklet describes how the pressures for increased mobility and flexibility are affecting young people's opportunities for finding decent jobs and homes. It also examines something of the wide range of responses that have developed at national and local level, many with the close involvement of young people themselves. (Published in all Community languages).

SY-53-89-279-EN-C   ECU 5.00

New Technology in the Public Service (1986)

This report focusses on the impact of technology on structures and functions in selected areas of the public service which offer a personal service to the public, for example social security payment offices and local employment agencies. It illustrates the effects of new technology on the employees of public agencies and the quality of service given to the public. The aims of and the process of planning for new technology are also considered. (Published in EN, FR, DE,DA,IT,NL,GR).

SX-46-86-185-EN-C   ECU 7.89

Technological Development: Options for the Future (1990)

The questions concerning how new technology can be implemented effectively, and how its impact on employees, customers and others can be made as beneficial as possible, have been studied for 10 years by the Foundation, and its findings are presented in this publication. The Foundation's research has covered engineering and other industrial sectors, banking and insurance, retailing, and the public services. It has considered new technology in production, in process operations, and in the office and has discussed its implications for managers, workers and customers as well as patients in health care. (Published in English only).

SY-53-88-293-EN-C   ECU 60.00

Meeting the Needs of the Elderly (1987)

This report, which consolidates 10 national studies, is based on an enquiry into public, private and voluntary provision for improving the living conditions of the elderly. It focuses on informal care and contacts in the family or with neighbours and friends; the services of volunteers, whether through voluntary organisations or with statutory services, and not least, action by and mutual aid among the elderly themselves. (Published in EN, FR, DE, IT).

SY-50-87-493-EN-C   ECU 10.50

The above, and all Foundation publications, are available upon request from the Official Sales Offices of the European Communities, the addresses of which are listed at the end of this publication.

Information booklet series

No. 1 Visual display unit workplaces: emerging trends and problems

No. 2 Safety in hazardous wastes

No. 3 Providing information about urban services

No. 4 Living conditions in urban Europe

No. 5 Commuting in the European Community

No. 6 The reporting of occupational accidents and diseases in the European Community

No. 7 Participation in technological change
(Out of print; replaced by Information Booklet No.11)

No. 8 Adapting shiftwork arrangements. Why and How?

No. 9 New technology in manufacturing industry

No. 10 Office automation

No. 11 Participation in change: New technology and the role of the employee involvement

No. 12 Taking action against long-term unemployment in Europe

No. 13 Working for a better environment: The role of the Social Partners

No. 14 Growing up and leaving Home

No. 15 Public Services: Working for the consumer

The above, and all Foundation publications, are available upon request from the Official Sales Offices of the European Communities, the addresses of which are listed at the end of this publication.